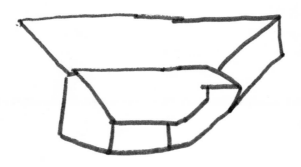

# MONEY MAGNETISM:
## How to Grow
## Rich Beyond Your
## Wildest Dreams

*NORVELL*

Parker Publishing Company, Inc.     West Nyack, New York

## Other Books by Norvell

*Cosmic Magnetism: The Miracle of the Magic Power Circle*
*Exorcism: Overcome Black Magic with White Magic*
*How to Develop Your Psychic Power for Health, Wealth, and Security*
*How to Train Your Child's Subconscious Mind for Health, Wealth, and Happiness*
*Meta-Physics: New Dimensions of the Mind*
*Mind Cosmology*
*The Miracle Power of Transcendental Meditation*
*Norvell's Dynamic Mental Laws for Successful Living*
*The Occult Sciences: How to Get What You Want through Your Occult Powers*
*The $100,000 Dream and How to Make It Come True*
*Universal Secrets of Telecosmic Power*

©1975 By
PARKER PUBLISHING COMPANY, INC.
West Nyack, New York

Library of Congress Cataloging in Publication Data

Norvell.
    Money magnetism.

    1.  Success.  2.  Occult sciences.  I.  Title.
BJ1611.2.N67              131'.32              74-13373
ISBN 0-13-600338-9

Printed in the United States of America

# How to Attract Big Money Using This Book

Magnetism flows through your brain and body, as well as throughout time and space. Your mind can be magnetized with ideas that cause it to attract whatever you want.

Just as your mind sends out magnetic wavelengths to cause you to desire food when you are hungry, so too, your mind can be magnetized with wavelengths of desire to attract money, possessions, friends, love, happiness, gifts, talents and everything you need to give you a perfect life here and now.

This book gives you a proven step-by-step system for supercharging the powerful, money-pulling poles of your mind with money magnetism—the same power that geniuses of the past have used and our modern millionaires employ every day *But here's the good part.* You don't have to be a genius to put these secrets to work. Once you discover the simple methods and practices in this book, you too can magnetize your brain centers with ideas that irresistibly attract—almost as if by magic—money, lands, possessions, jewels, houses, friends—all the rich, fine and glittering things in life.

This book is filled with real-life accounts of ordinary people—just like yourself—who've used these secrets to bring a floodtide of riches into their lives. You, too, have only to stir up the "mental filings" in your mind. The magnetic force is *already there.* You have only to use this book and, by so doing, turn on the switch that releases an unending stream of abundant riches—beginning *right now.*

But don't take my word for it. Let me prove this to you.

Here are just twenty ways this book will help you become rich and successful beyond your wildest dreams:

1. You will learn how to find the Hidden Vein of Gold within your subconscious mind, tap it and start the flow of money into your life immediately. Discover the method for building success and money habits that can make you rich.

Find out about the Money Chest that is within your subconscious mind and release its power to bring you from $1,000 to $1,000,000. See how one man used this secret power to build a $10,000,000-a-year business. Learn how a woman was guided to a round-the-world tour when she had no money and there met a millionaire, who later married her. Learn about the money pump exercise that can start the flow of golden ideas that can make you rich. This priceless information is revealed in Chapter 6.

2. Discover for yourself the royal road to riches that is marked by definite signposts that you can follow to fame and fortune. Learn how to use your desires for magnetizing money. Discover the power of creative imagination and learn how great people have used it to build fortunes. One young man used this secret to magnetize $85,000 through his first novel. You will be shown how to use the golden substance of time and convert it into fame and fortune. One woman with three children, used this power to make $5,000,000 through her writing. Discover the money-building habits that the first Rockefeller used to build a great financial empire. All this and more is revealed in Chapter 4.

3. You can build the same money magnetism that rich people have used throughout history to become powerful and rich. Learn the dynamic laws under which money operates and how rich people stir magnetic centers in their minds which irresistibly attract a steady flow of money. Find out the seven money master motives that can bring you a fortune. Learn how to build money awareness by practicing with simulated money

from \$1,000 to \$100,000 bills, until you build a true million-dollar consciousness. Discover the 10 secrets used by the world's richest people and then set about magnetizing as much money as you think you will need for a lifetime. This secret power was used by Carnegie, Vanderbilt, Onassis, Howard Hughes, J. Paul Getty and other millionaires. Chapter 1 will give you the startling details about how to magnetize a fortune.

4. You can build a million-dollar consciousness and begin in this moment to think, talk, look and act like a millionaire! This is the beginning of your moment of truth, for when you discover this priceless secret you not only enrich your higher mind with money magnetism but you start the flow of money *at once!* Learn the secret vow of riches that all millionaires make and then begin to tap the same cosmic cornucopia of riches that all rich people have tapped. One man took a vow of riches and promised his wife that on their twentieth wedding anniversary he would give her \$25,000. He gave her a check for that amount to deposit in the bank at that time. Exactly 20 years later she cashed the check he had given her when they first married! He then had \$1,000,000 in his bank account!

Learn how you can create a scrapbook of riches. Put into that scrapbook the car, the house, the jewelry, the stocks or land you want to own. Then be guided by your million-dollar consciousness to the building of your fortune. The information of how you can do this is given fully in Chapter 3.

5. There are Golden Nuggets lying just beneath the surface of your consciousness which you may bring to the surface and these can make you rich. Your subconscious mind is the golden goose that lays the golden eggs of riches. You can learn how to program your subconscious mind to release all the money you will ever need. You can tap this power to develop your creative talents that can make you rich. A girl who needed money was guided to a secret hiding place in a dream, where her dead father had concealed \$15,000 in cash. A man discovered \$92,000 hidden

in an upholstered chair; he received the information from a woman who came to him in a dream. There are Golden Nuggets lying all around you in cash and ideas, which you can tap when you once learn this priceless secret. A woman used this secret to find a position that brought her $15,000 a year. Another woman asked for $100,000 and got it by being guided to a real estate investment. Learn how you can trigger these Golden Nuggets from your subconscious mind. This priceless information is given in Chapter 2.

6. The law of the double return can help you double your luck and bring you financial independence. This law works in nature to produce abundant crops when you plant a seed. Learn the secret of the Money Pyramid and how to invoke it whenever you need money. Discover the power of the Golden Law of Alchemy to increase your money supply. A young man used this secret and won a half-million dollars in stakes to breed and raise horses. The Cosmic Law of Projection can bring you millions when you release creative ideas. A young man made over a million dollars in cosmetology by using this secret. This method for doubling your money and doubling your luck is given in detail in Chapter 8.

7. Do you want to start the flow of unlimited riches? You can literally open the Cosmic Storehouse of Riches and obtain an unlimited supply of money and things of value when you use the secret power of the Law of Vibration bank of riches. Learn of the cosmic law of duplication that nature uses to create a field of wheat or an apple orchard. You can start this process of unlimited creative power in your life by simply using certain commands that will open the invisible doors to the storehouse of treasures in the universe. One man used this method to start a business where he received $2,000 in the first month from letters that came to his home. He programmed his subconscious mind to bring him riches without ever leaving his house. Learn about the Cosmic Catalogue from which you can order a color

TV set, a fur coat, jewels, a car and other things of value you desire. A woman obtained a fur coat worth $1,500 and a new refrigerator, a bedroom suite and a color TV set through this secret method. You will find this Money Magnetism formula in Chapter 9.

8. Your brain is a money mint and can turn out any denomination of currency that is stamped on its sensitive surface. The U.S. Mint turns out copper, nickle, silver or gold coins, depending on the imprint on a die. Likewise your mind can stamp out the currency or value that is stamped on its surface with magnetism. Learn how to make your mind a money-making machine. Use the 10 magnetic programmers to release money in your life. A young Greek girl used this secret power and attracted a job with a wealthy old woman; later she met a rich shipping magnate's son and married him. Learn how you can use this method to magnetize money. You will find this amazing secret in Chapter 7.

9. You can learn how to project money magnetism in such a way that you can influence and control rich people, making them want to help you. Learn of the 10 ways by which you can meet rich people and influence them. One young man used this method and earned $10,000 for one idea for a TV commercial that was bought by an advertising firm. Find out the playgrounds of the wealthy and learn how you can get in with them. One man arranged a meeting with a famous industrialist and got an order for $90,000 worth of merchandise! A clerk in a department store used this secret formula and was commissioned by Andrew Carnegie to buy up furnishings for his famous castle in Scotland. Truman Capote, Tennesee Williams and Gore Vidal actually use this secret in meeting and associating with famous people in international society. A girl was left $50,000 in the will of a rich woman because she invoked this money magnetism formula. Find out how you can become rich

by projecting money magnetism. This information is given in Chapter 5.

10. Why do some people become rich while others remain poverty-stricken all their lives? The answer is that rich people build the million-dollar personality that magnetizes their auras with money know-how. Learn how to change your mental image from one of failure and poverty to one of self-confidence, importance and success. Learn the Mirror Money Treatment that can make you worth $50,000 a year in salary. Build the magnetic money aura that will make others want to give you riches and abundance. Discover the power of the Magic Circle of money success that all wealthy people have. The famous movie stars of Hollywood, TV and the Broadway stage all use this dynamic principle of the Magic Circle. You can acquire the same power and build the million-dollar personality of the Magic Circle by studying carefully and applying the principles given in Chapter 11.

11. There are 15 science-of-success secrets that are used by the world's richest people to bring them fame and fortune. Learn how to use your powers of magnetism and persuasion to influence others and to win them to your side. Discover the method by which you can put money to work for you and achieve a fortune. Discover the 11 basic human needs and how you can fill these and build a fortune for yourself. See the golden opportunities that are all around you and which you may tap by knowing these science-of-success secrets. The art of personification can imprint your subconscious mind with riches and make you achieve success. Concentration and visualization can be used by you to make a fortune. These secrets for achieving riches are given in Chapter 13.

12. There is a golden stairway that can lead you to fame and fortune. Learn of the ten positive forces that can magnetize your mind and direct you up that golden ladder of dreams to success and fulfillment. Use emotionalized desire to guide you to riches. Use creative imagination to unfold ideas that can make

you rich beyond your wildest dreams. Learn how a housewife built a million-dollar fortune through her imagination. Discover how to use the power of faith to develop the million-dollar ideas that can make you rich. You can use these positive programming techniques that will bring you success and riches. They are all given in Chapter 10.

13. Can your higher psychic centers be developed to guide you to fame and fortune? You will be shown how you can use your psychic hunches to bring you wealth. One man made millions in the stock market by following his intuition. Bernard Baruch turned $35,000 into a million-dollar fortune by using a psychic hunch that a particular stock would go down. You can create a psychic whirlpool for attracting infinite riches through your psychic centers. A woman followed her psychic hunch to enter a cake-baking contest and won $5,000 as first prize. This priceless information on how you can use your psychic hunches is revealed in Chapter 12.

14. Rich people automatically know how to use 20 magnetic money energizers that crystallize their ideas and turn them into gold. All things are created first in your mind and then released to the outer world through your creative actions. Learn of the 20 simple magnetic money energizers that can align your conscious and subconscious minds, causing them to release a steady flow of money-making ideas. This great secret is given for the first time in Chapter 14.

15. There is a Psychic Money Bank that you can learn to tap that will bring you everything you desire in life. This includes money, jewels, houses, land, stocks, cars and other things of value. Learn about the Cosmic Laws that can produce these treasures for you. This Psychic Money Bank can be tapped through a mystical regimen that comes from the Far East. Learn a few simple money chants that you can use in meditation to start the flow of money into your hands. Ask this higher psychic mind how to get anywhere from $5,000 to $1,000,000. It knows the answers to all things. A man sold a million-dollar

property through this psychic guidance. Discover this method for tapping the Psychic Money Bank to bring you infinite riches. It is revealed in Chapter 15.

16. How can you avoid the negative type of magnetism that attracts failure and poverty? Learn how to program the winning statements in your subconscious mind to win love, friends and money. One man was negatively programmed with the words BORN TO LOSE, which were tattooed on his arm, and his life was one of constant failures. Another man used this programming in a positive way and he became a two-star admiral. Another man used this system to go into a business partnership with a man in the building industry where he stands to make $100,000 a year. Learn how to command and control the positive forces of your life and make them bring you riches. Discover these secrets of positive magnetism in Chapter 7.

17. There is magic power in believing and receiving your good and through this regimen you can magnetize riches and abundance. You can invoke this magic power of faith to increase your talents, to bring you money and to develop creative gifts and talents that can make you a fortune. A man and his wife used this formula to receive the sum of $5,000 from an unexpected source. If you desire sums of money from $10,000 to $100,000 you can use this formula and you will attract it over a period of time. Use the prayer of thanksgiving and blessings to increase your good. Activate the flow of money by using the great cosmic law of giving and you will receive friendship, love, health, happiness and riches. The method for doing this is given in Chapter 16.

18. There are seven dynamic money laws that can make you rich. Use money as a symbol and turn your golden Midas touch into riches and success by respecting money and not hating it. This power of magnetic attraction works in the soil to bring us fruits and vegetables, lumber and chemicals, gold and oil, coal and silver and other things of value. Learn how to use

this same magnetic source to obtain all the things you desire in your life. Study the lives of such men as Ford, Vanderbilt, Rockefeller, Onassis, J. Paul Getty, W. Clement Stone, Morganthau, J.P. Morgan and other rich men. These interesting and dynamic money laws are given in Chapter 17.

19. Learn how you can create a Money Syphon, wherever you are, even if you live in the desert, to bring you untold riches.

A man who lived in a poverty-stricken village in Greece used this psychic Money Syphon to bring him what was equivalent to a fortune. How does this psychic Money Syphon work in nature? It brings you coffee from Brazil, eggs from a farm, milk from a cow you never met, bacon from pigs that have been raised especially for you, bread from wheat raised in the Midwest and all these people are working for you to bring you a simple breakfast every morning without your conscious effort. Turn this psychic Money Syphon into a channel to also bring you money, jewels, furs, cars, land and other treasures you desire. This stupendous secret alone could convert your life into one of riches and abundance. All this and more is revealed for you in Chapter 15.

20. You will be shown how to use simple statements of creative action that will program your subconscious mind at once to wealth and power. You can motivate your higher mind to release ideas that can make you rich. You can invoke the law of the harvest that brings money and possessions. You will be shown how to use the money energizer statement of I ELE-VATE to raise your levels of achievement and increase your productivity and mental power. A woman used this simple programming method and changed her entire life. She obtained a better job and married happily, when formerly she could not attract work or love. A junk dealer used this system of money programming and built a business of $7,000,000 a year. He now lives in a mansion and is driving in a chauffeured limousine

and has everything he ever desired. You can tap this same astounding power by studying the principles given in Chapter 14.

There's a whole world of wonderful, rich things out there for *you*. If you don't get your share, somebody else will—and they'll be using money magnetism to get what is rightfully yours. You can magnetize and attract whatever you want. It's all in knowing how to do it. Turn the page and take the first step that will transform your life and bring you the wondrous things that up until now you thought were only the stuff of dreams

NORVELL

# Table of Contents

# 10 SIMPLE SECRETS USED
# BY THE WORLD'S RICHEST
# PEOPLE TO MAGNETIZE MONEY

# 1

**M** oney is a man-made commodity. In itself it has no value, but is a symbol of man's creative ideas, his labor, and his time and effort. To magnetize and attract money or its equivalents in goods and possessions, you must understand certain laws that govern money and its accumulation.

A man once discovered a gold mine in Nevada, in the early days when there were few cars. He ran out of water and as he lay dying he scribbled on a piece of paper, "I would give everything in my gold mine for one cup of water!"

Money is important, for with it you can buy the things you need to give you comfort, health, happiness and security. But money in itself when accumulated for its own sake, seldom brings happiness or peace of mind.

In learning how to make your mind a money magnet, we snall find out the basic economic laws that govern and control money, but also the ways in which you can magnetize and attract to yourself the equivalents of money, such as houses, lands, cars, jewels, fur coats, trips to Europe, education for your children, and other things of value. The same magnetic principle applies to these money equivalents and many times you will magnetize and attract these things even though you do not have a great deal of money.

The law of magnetism applies to all created things. All atoms and molecules are held together by the invisible flow of magnetism. When you want to attract something it is necessary that you cause your mind to project magnetism to the outer world and magnetize what you wish to attract.

You will see this law of magnetism, or attraction, at work in every sphere of action. Golfers join a club where they can meet others interested in that sport. Race track enthusiasts gather by the thousands to bet on horses; they are driven there by the magnetic law of attraction. Ski enthusiasts flock to their winter sport under this same law. You magnetize and attract what you are most interested in.

In this chapter we shall learn how magnetism can be used to attract money to you; how your mind can actually be charged like a magnet with rich ideas that can reach out in time and space and motivate the invisible atoms and molecules and marshall them into lines of energy that cause you to do the things that make you successful and rich.

## THE FOUR DIFFERENT FORMS OF MAGNETISM THAT EXIST

In learning how to make your mind a money magnet, it is important that you first learn of the four different forms of magnetism that exist in the world. You can then choose that particular form that you desire for attracting whatever you choose.

1. Mental Magnetism
2. Physical Magnetism
3. Material Magnetism
4. Spiritual Magnetism

It is important for you to know which form of magnetism you will use to invoke the Law of Magnetic Attraction.

In a study of 10,000 famous and rich people throughout history over a period of 25 years, I discovered that the first and most important secret that was used by all of them to magnetize and attract money was that they built a powerful form of Mental Magnetism *by desiring money and the things that money can do.*

## THE 10 SECRETS USED BY THE WORLD'S RICHEST PEOPLE TO MAGNETIZE MONEY

### 1. A desire to do good for the world and help others

Desire for success creates Mental Magnetism and drives a person in the direction of that which he desires.

If you have an intense desire to succeed so you can do something of value for the world the chances are that you will attract all the money you need to fulfill that ambition perfectly.

The fortune of Andrew Carnegie was won by a poor immigrant boy who had a desire to help the expanding economy of his adopted country through a knowledge of steel making. Not only did Carnegie become one of the wealthiest men of his time, but he gave 1,200 public libraries to America, donated the cultural institute known as Carnegie Hall in New York City to the people, and also endowed the Carnegie Institute. It is estimated that he gave more than 500,000,000 dollars in charitable donations to the country that had made him rich!

Carnegie used all four forms of Magnetism given here: Mental magnetism—the desire to help others; physical magnetism, the stirring of creative power in his brain and body that gave him the strength and health to achieve his goal; material magnetism, the attraction to money, and its intelligent use when he had accumulated a fortune; and spiritual magnetism, in developing faith in the higher power that guided him to his life destiny, and the application of the spiritual principles of good, charity, love of humanity, and giving beauty to the world.

You can make your mind a money magnet by running this magnetic principle through the filaments of your brain: Look around you and see in what way you can create something that will benefit other people, something that will help humanity rise higher, suffer less, enjoy more, become greater, achieve higher goals, and then ask your subconscious mind to guide you to the work that can help you attain this magnetic goal. When you discover what it is, you can become rich and famous through this magnetic discovery.

### HOW A MAN BUILT A MULTIMILLION DOLLAR FORTUNE

A man named Dr. Thomas B. Welch was a church-going man who disliked liquor and wondered if he couldn't discover some substitute that would be as enjoyable as a drink without intoxicating people. With this magnetic thought to do good for humanity, he started to search for something he could use as a substitute for alcohol.

He lived in Vineland, New Jersey, where there were plenty of Concord grapes, so Dr. Welch began to squeeze grapes and put the juice into bottles. He began to give some of the bottles to his local church, and soon people were demanding Welch's grape juice. In a short time he was bottling hundreds of bottles of grape juice and selling it to stores. In a few short years Welch's grape juice became one of the biggest sellers in America and incidentally, made Dr. Welch and his family rich.

**2. You can make your mind a money magnet by releasing the power of your creative imagination**

The first man who saw a bird flying and imagined that man

would one day grow wings had a preview glimpse of the modern jet liner and man's flight to the moon and back!

When some ancient cave-dweller first saw a stone rolling down a hillside and imagined what it would be like to attach a round object to a cart, giving it mobility, the wheel was born. Scientists say the wheel was one of the greatest of all inventions and laid the foundation for our modern age of machines and industry.

You can create money magnetism within your mind by imagining what you will do to build a fortune. You can project the mental images of what you will do with your money; you can build your mental bank account and see money piling up, see yourself writing checks for things you want.

Sit down each day and build a sense of Money Awareness. Cut pieces of newspaper out the size of money, and mentally stack it, labelling each one $100,000, until you have built a stack of 1,000,000 dollars. As you build your money sense, you will be automatically using physical magnetism, and creating within your brain the desire and intense energy to *produce the money you have created in your imagination.*

## FORD BUILT A BILLION DOLLAR EMPIRE
## WITH THIS MAGNETIC SECRET

When Henry Ford imagined cars being created on an assembly line, he was invoking mental magnetism through his creative imagination and he was on his way to building a billion-dollar empire. One day Ford imagined a motor that was radically different from the motor of that day. He called in his engineers and told them he wanted them to produce a V-8 motor for his cars. They told him it couldn't be done. He told them to go away and keep trying until they accomplished it. Six months later they perfected the V-8 motor that revolutionized the motor industry and brought Ford additional millions.

### 3. Daring to dream big and wanting to achieve something great helps magnetize your mind centers with money power

Most of the great fortunes created by those whose lives I studied were the results of their daring to dream big. These people had unlimited vision and the courage to achieve the seemingly impossible dream.

Hilton had a dream in which his hotels encircled the globe. He achieved this dream through his daring to believe it was possible.

Onassis dreamed of a fleet of ships that would visit every port on earth, and a struggling deck hand who worked for others achieved a billion-dollar fortune.

Leonardo da Vinci dreamed of a flying machine, and invented the world's first motorless plane. He wrote on this design these prophetic words, "Man shall one day grow wings." Now the impossible dream of reaching the moon and the planets is on the road to fulfillment. We have conquered the moon and soon will be visiting other planets.

Dare to dream the big dream; see yourself rich and powerful. Visualize yourself living in a beautiful home; see the car you want to drive as being luxurious; visualize yourself owning your own business and becoming a millionaire.

### 4. Unimpeded vision of the future with its vast potentials has accounted for the building of many great fortunes in the past

See your possibilities as being infinite, no matter your present limitations of education or environment.

Many people who live in small cities often complain, "How can one achieve riches when one's opportunities are limited by living in a small town or city?"

A man named Peter Kuyper lived in a little village named Pella, in Iowa. It has few oppo tunities to get rich, so this man began to search elsewhere for his opportunities. One day he read an ad in a big city newspaper telling of a business opportunity which required a small investment.

It was a business making a rolling window screen. At the time this concern had only three employees. Pete Kuyper, with his expanded vision, decided to move the manufacturing firm to his small town, giving employment to his fellow citizens. Within a short time Kuyper's business grew and expanded until he had 500 employees and the factory spread over 200,000 square feet. It put the town of Pella, Iowa on the map. In fact, Kuyper was so proud of his home town that he called his products Pella Rolscreens, Pella Venetian blinds, and Pella casement windows.

### 5. Find a basic human need and then fill that need

You will receive not only riches and recognition, but you will arouse Mental Magnetism because you are working to give something of value to the world.

### 6. Create something that will help beautify the world and you will attract a fortune

A man named Henry Rosenfeld, using this magnetic secret, decided he would make stylish dresses available to all women. He had tremendous competition but he decided to turn out gowns that retailed for as high as $100 at rock-bottom prices. His first big order came from New York's Best and Co., when he sold them an order for 5,000 flannel gowns for only $9.75 each. He didn't even have an office in which to write up that first order! From that beginning he went on to build a business that grossed $15,000,000 a year, and he became one of the biggest men in the dress business.

Rosenfeld likes to tell the story of how he programmed himself to become a millionaire. When he was only nine years of age he promised his mother that by the time he was 35 years old he would be a millionaire! He said the happiest day of his life was on his thirty-fifth birthday, when he was able to show his mother a bank book with the sum of $1,000,000 in his name!

One man used this magnetic desire to bring beauty to women. He got the idea of bringing home permanent waves to them without the fuss and bother of sitting in a beauty parlor, and paying from $15 to $30 for a permanent wave. This man had only $1,000 when he hit on the idea of making a home beauty kit that would give women good permanent waves at home. He called his product Toni Home Permanent and within a short time he was selling 2,000,000 kits a month. *Life* magazine told the fascinating story of this man who later sold his company for $20,000,000!

### 7. One of the quickest ways to magnetize your brain centers is through the expression of faith

Have faith in yourself first; know that you will attract the fortune you desire.

Second, have faith in your product, for only when you believe in something with all your heart and soul can you inspire others to buy that product.

A very inferior shoe salesman in New York could hardly sell a pair of shoes. He was timid, negative and constantly felt that he was not impressing his customer with the necessity of buying his product. He began to study these principles of success and after three months he decided that he had more to give to the world than he could in such a limited field. He saw an ad one day telling of a school that trained men to be supersalesmen in insurance.

He took this course, and began to have the faith in himself that he could become one of the best salesmen in that field. Within six months from the time he finished his course he was working for one of the biggest life insurance companies in the world! He had such confidence in himself that he was selected to go to branches of the company all over America and train salesmen! His salary jumped from a few thousand a year into the $45,000 bracket! Faith changed his whole approach to life and opened his eyes to his hidden potentials for greater success.

**8. One of the most powerful methods for building money magnetism is to use the power of visualization and project the mental images of the things you want in your life**

This art of Fantasia, as it is called in Italian, is a mental exercise in which you sit quietly and hold in your mind the things that you want to do.

If it is a large sum of money like $10,000 or more, you sit for a few moments visualizing yourself getting the money, and then you mentally spend it on the things you want. This art of Fantasia is different from the mere act of imagining what it would be like to have $10,000. In the art of Fantasia you mentally project *yourself* into the future scene and actually experience the emotional impact of how you would feel and act if you suddenly had that money. You might visualize yourself winning it through a lottery, or by entering a contest. You see yourself putting it into the bank; you mentally draw on that money and see yourself buying the things you desire.

The art of Fantasia works miracles, for it seems to trigger some subconscious power that causes you to do the things you are fantasizing.

**9. Most of the world's richest men magnetized their brain centers through the quality of resourcefulness**

They did not always accept the limitations of their times and the many discouragements they ran into. They forged ahead, using resourcefulness to show them new ways to achieve their high goals.

**10. One of the most magnetic properties which you can put into your mind is enthusiasm**

If you feel enthusiastic about something, that emotion will reach out and magnetize others with the same quality of enthusiasm. Each day practice projecting enthusiasm in your personality. When you approach a prospect to make a sale, show your enthusiasm and you will arouse the person you are trying to sell, as enthusiasm is contagious. When you share an experience with another person, be enthusiastic and he will usually respond with the same emotion.

## POINTS TO REMEMBER

1. Money is a man-made commodity, subject to the laws of economics as well as to the law of magnetic attraction.
2. The law of gravity or magnetism works to keep the heavenly bodies in their orbits, and this same power works mentally, physically, materially and spiritually to bring you whatever you need to fulfill your destiny perfectly.
3. The richest people in the world are those who stir magnetic centers in the consciousness of others through service, or giving something of value to the world.
4. The love of money is the root of all evil, not money itself. Desire money for the good you can do and it will furnish you with a powerful magnet that will attract all the money you need.
5. Use the magnetism of desire to bring you money and make you a magnetic center for creative ideas that can make you rich.
6. Dr. Welch built a million-dollar fortune by having a desire to give a nonalcoholic beverage to the world. He developed Welch's grape juice.

7. Release the creative power of your imagination to start the flow of money magnetism to your higher mind centers.

8. Build money awareness by practicing on cut-out pieces of paper and labeling them $100,000 each, until you have magnetized a million dollars.

9. A higher master motive than merely wanting money can magnetize your brain centers and cause you to attract fame, fortune and success in every part of your life.

10. Expand your consciousness to big things through the big dream of success and riches.

11. A small town man with a big vision built one of the biggest firms in his town that employed 500 people and put the town of Pella, Iowa on the map.

12. A desire to beautify the world has built some of the world's greatest fortunes through beauty products, home products, architecture, manufacturing of cars, and dozens of other items that give usefulness and beauty to the world.

13. Use the magnetic property of faith to bring you money and fame.

# HOW TO RELEASE THE GOLDEN NUGGETS OF YOUR MIND THAT CAN MAKE YOU RICH

# 2

**Y**our mind possesses a creative power that can convert your thoughts into a stream of Golden Nuggets that can make you successful, famous and rich. The power to change your creative thoughts into outer material riches and success lies within your own subconscious mind.

This higher intelligence knows everything there is to know about you and your hidden potentials for greatness. It can guide you unerringly to the fulfillment of your big money goals and bring you financial security and fulfillment of your every wish.

This chapter reveals this secret power for releasing the Golden Nuggets of your mind that can make you rich.

If you tell your subconscious mind, "I want you to bring me ideas to make a million dollars," your subconscious will know whether you actually possess that ability or not. If you do not have the capacity for making a million dollars it will send through ideas that can bring you as much money as you are capable of visualizing.

You can build your creative mind power to encompass as

much money as you want, but you must first be sure that you have the capacity to understand how much you really need and can honestly produce.

This is the reason why most people are limited in their ability to attract a fortune. They have had little or no business training; sometimes they are uneducated and ignorant, and they consciously know that they cannot attract the large fortune they desire. Such people are doomed to disappointment when they try to become rich. They soon give up trying and fall back into their old habit patterns of thinking in terms of small salaries and limited luxuries.

## HOW TO PROGRAM THE SUBCONSCIOUS MIND WITH GOLDEN NUGGETS

You have undoubtedly read the fairy tale about the goose that laid the golden eggs. The farmer was delighted at first to receive these golden eggs each day, but as time passed, his greed got the best of him and he thought instead of taking only one egg a day, why not kill the goose and get all the golden eggs at one time. Of course, when he did, that was the end of the golden goose and there were no more golden eggs!

Your subconscious mind can be programmed with Golden Nuggets of thought that will produce a perpetual stream of golden ideas that you can turn into cash or its equivalents.

Your subconscious mind can be programmed with these golden ideas each day, until it actually becomes a rich repository of money-making ideas that bring you instant cash or the equivalents of money.

The power of your higher mind is stupendous. It knows all secrets; it knows things you do not know. In research done recently by scientists, it is now found possible for your higher mind to reach out, even when you sleep, and contact some higher mind, which mystics call Cosmic Mind, and learn secrets that have been hidden for years.

A young woman had such an experience recently. She had taken care of her invalid father for five years. When he died suddenly, she was left without money on which to live. She was confident, however, that she would be taken care of. She went to bed one night and her father appeared to her, as in a dream, and talked to her, "I know you are worried about money," he said. "But I left you well provided for. In the old chest of drawers in the living room you will find a hidden compartment. Put your hand in there and you will find money I have hidden over the years to take care of you."

The girl awakened, and went to the old chest of drawers. She put her hand in the secret compartment and there found a big roll of bills in denominations from $20 to $100. Her father had not trusted banks, having lost money in the Depression days and he had deposited $15,000 in cash in that chest of drawers! The girl's subconscious mind had been told, in a dream, of this secret hiding place!

**Golden Nugget No. 1: I will make $100,000 or more.**

When you have programmed this golden nugget into your subconscious mind by repeating it at least 10 times, you will then program the following statements into your higher mind.

> I desire $100,000 or more to fulfill my money goals in the immediate future. I wish to receive some big idea that will reveal to me the method by which I can begin the flow of gold immediately to meet all my needs.

Write this subconscious mind motivator down on a filing card. Keep this card where you can read it every day, morning noon and night, preferably in your pocket. You may also tape it on your wall where you can see it frequently, reminding your subconscious mind that you expect to receive vital money information that will guide you to the sums of money you desire.

> **Golden Nugget No. 2: I shall become a big success in my own business, in which I shall make $50,000 or more a year.**

Then write on a filing card the following subconscious motivators:

> I wish to be shown what talent I have and how I can commercialize on this talent by going into my own business where I can create something valuable and useful to the world. I project my own office, my own staff of workers and I see my efforts being rewarded with big success

Note: If you wish some specific business you must name the type of business. Examples include: I wish to become a big interior decorator. I wish to be a successful landscape architect. I would like my own beauty parlor. I would like to open my own restaurant, or bar, or barber shop. Whatever it is you feel you should do, tell your subconscious mind specifically in simple words and the subconscious mind will program it within the computerlike structure of its higher mind, and release the information to your conscious mind that will lead you into the exact type of business you desire.

If you do not know the type of business you would like to open, leave it up to your own subconscious mind, for it knows even better than you do your unique talents and how you can find the pathway to riches through your subconscious mind. An example from my files will prove this point fully.

A woman who was working as a secretary for a big manufacturing concern grew tired of working for a small weekly salary. After learning how she could program her subconscious mind through my classes in New York City, she began to use this method to go into her own business. But what could she do? She knew of no specific talent she had, and had only been trained for secretarial work.

This woman wrote down on her programming sheet the following Golden Nugget and fed it into her subconscious mind every day for four weeks, using only 5 minutes three times a day for her subconscious programming work.

> I wish to be shown how to go into a productive business. I want to make the sum of $15,000 or more a year. I wish to have enough money to take care of my two children, to buy a new home in the country, to own a new car, and to have security for the future.

After writing down these Golden Nuggets and putting them into her subconscious mind, she awaited results confidently, expectant of success.

One day when she was taking a trip on an airplane going to Chicago on some business for her company, she sat next to a man who began talking to her about his work. He was a traveling sales representative for a large manufacturing concern specializing in household products. His company was opening up new offices in different cities and needed responsible representatives that could interview employees, apportion districts for salesmen, and act as agents in certain localities. Before they had reached Chicago, this man was so impressed by the young woman's ability that he hired her to take charge of the new office in her New York area. From that beginning she went on to making commissions and salary that brought her more than the $15,000 a year she had programmed her subconscious mind for! Now this woman has embarked on a sales training program, where she instructs hundreds of salesmen for her company on the principal points to stress in selling their products. From this new venture she hopes to soon be in the $50,000 a year class!

**Golden Nugget No. 3: I wish to be shown how to make money through real estate, stocks and bonds, or other investments.**

Many big fortunes have been built through investments in real estate, the stock market, gold mines, oil wells and other investments in natural resources. This type of subconscious programming should be started early in life and continued until you achieve the fortune you desire. Here is the form of subconscious conditioning that this requires. Say these words over several times, and then write them down on a filing card looking at them at least two or three times a day, until your subconscious mind is programmed with these golden nuggets for money

I wish to become a successful real estate operator, or to be shown how to invest in the right stocks or other resources that can bring me a fortune in the future.

A man who used this type of subconscious programming in Los Angeles, California, was guided by his higher mind to buy land in San Fernando Valley before it had become so expensive. From his early investment in corner lots, he later made two million dollars!

A woman lecture member in New York City used this same subconscious mind programming technique to secure her future. She put down that she wished to have $100,000 or more through land development and through stock market investments. She had little money to start, but one day she went on a vacation to the Bahamas, and there she found a land development that she could invest in with only a little money and payments each month, which she could afford. She bought property overlooking the waterfront. The Grand Bahamas became a big tourist attraction a few years later and she realized $50,000 from that investment! This same woman did the same thing with property in Arizona and Albuquerque, New Mexico, investing in corner lots, with small down payments. She held these five years and realized a profit of more than $25,000 on each investment! But her subconscious mind, the goose that lays the golden eggs had not finished giving her rich dividends for her mental work; she had also asked that she be shown how to invest in stocks that would make her successful.

One day a man who was concerned with selling her some of the land in Arizona, which she bought, told her she should buy a particular stock. It was selling for only $2 a share. She bought one thousand shares and held it a short time; this stock had a phenomenal rise, going up to $60 a share. She sold it just a little under the peak and made thousands of dollars more! Now this woman has retired in her beautiful home near Phoenix, Arizona, to enjoy the financial security she won through subconscious mind programming!

> **Golden Nugget No. 4: I wish to develop some great creative talent that will permit me to give something special to the world.**

Most of the world's talented people started out in life with ordinary goals. Only when they programmed their subconscious minds with extraordinary ideas did they begin to discover the special talent they possessed which could bring them fame and fortune.

To program this golden nugget into your subconscious mind write down the following conditioner on a filing card and look at it several times a day, until it automatically triggers some reaction from your higher mind which will start you on the road to fulfillment of your desire.

> I would like to become an __artist__ . (Here it is important that you write down the specific talent you want to develop. You may select as many as four or five, for generally, when your subconscious mind releases one gift, it automatically triggers other talents you possessed, but which you had not

yet recognized.) You may select any of the following gifts, or make up your own list: Writing stories or poetry or TV dramas. Interior Decorating. Inventing. Composing music. Advertising. Singing, acting or dancing. Playing an instrument. Dress designer. Architect. Public speaking.

After you have chosen the talents you want to develop write down the following subconscious conditioners:

I know that my subconscious mind can give me guidance as to how to develop this special talent. I ask that I be shown how to release the golden nuggets of creative thought that can make me famous, rich and successful.

When you have completed this subconscious conditioner, read it over several times a day, and then sit daily and wait for instructions from your higher mind as to what steps you should take to bring your creative talents to full maturity.

A top dress designer for Hollywood movie stars was once a student of mine when I lectured in that city. She is now a top dress designer, having been nominated three times for an Oscar for best designer. This young lady had worked as a waitress until she learned how to project the Golden Nugget of thought that she could become a great designer. She now makes a salary of $50,000 a year!

Golden Nugget No. 5: I wish to receive money or its equivalents in rewards, jewels, houses, cars, land or other things of value through the use of my present abilities.

Very often you can program your subconscious mind to release money or its equivalents instantly, wherever you are, and with whatever abilities you now possess. This means that you do not need to wait for some future, distant day to be a success, nor do you need to develop an unusual talent. Using the tools of mind you now possess, your subconscious mind can show you how to start the instantaneous flow of riches into your life with this Golden Nugget of thought.

Sit quietly and concentrate your mind power on the following subconscious conditioner when you desire the rewards just given.

> I wish to now trigger instant action from my subconscious mind. I want the sum of $500 for my immediate expenses. (Here you may substitute the sum that you actually have faith in and that you really need at once.) I desire a beautiful home of my own in the immediate future. I wish to own a car, beautiful clothing, jewels, and household furnishings that I need. I want to have a color TV set, air conditioner, a hi-fi set, a tape recorder, a big refrigerator and other material objects.

After you have programmed your subconscious mind with these conditioners, read the list over every day until you begin to see results. Do not become discouraged and give up! You may not have any money in the bank and you may not know how you could possibly receive the items you have put down on your Golden Nugget Ledger, but believe that somehow you will be the recipient of the gifts you have requested from your higher mind.

A student of mine in New York City put down on her list that she wanted a beautiful mink coat. It was cold in winter and she decided she should own a warm coat, but she had no money with which to buy such a coat. However, she wrote it down on her subconscious list of things she desired and confidently awaited results.

Within one week a very wealthy woman called an agency and asked for a practical nurse to be sent to help in her home. Her aged husband was very sick and required constant medical attention. This student of mine had taken a course in practical nursing and worked on special cases, but she did not make much money. She responded to the call from the nursing agency, who often sent her out on cases. She was delighted to find that her employer lived on Park Avenue in a luxury apartment. One cold February night, as the nurse was putting on her cloth coat to go home, the wealthy woman said to her, "Why, it's bitter cold out; you'll freeze with that thin coat!"

She went to a closet in her bedroom and returned with a beautiful mink coat that must have cost $5,000 when new. She said, "Here, I want you to have this coat. It's like new, as I seldom wear it. My husband bought me a new one for Christmas and I want you to have this."

The nurse had her fur coat that she had projected in her subconscious mind conditioner and it had not cost her a cent!

Golden Nugget No. 6: I have a desire to help my family, to educate my children, to give them a beautiful home environment and security for the future.

This Golden Nugget can be programmed into your subconscious mind and it will serve as the motivating force in back of your every act to make money or be successful.

Thousands of new inventions, creative ideas and money-making discoveries have been released from the subconscious mind under the impetus of this subconscious conditioner.

Write down the following words on a filing card to trigger this automatic action for bringing your family benefits.

I wish to help my family live a better life. I desire for them a higher education and opportunities to become successful. I wish to receive inspiration for ideas that will bring me monetary and other forms of success so I may give them financial and emotional security in the future.

A man was watching his wife open a can in the kitchen one

evening. The can opener, one of the old-fashioned kind, slipped and cut her hand. The man searched for a piece of cloth with which to bind the wound. Finally, he fashioned a clumsy bandage and applied it, realizing, however, that it could easily infect his wife's hand.

He found himself thinking: If only there were some ready-made, sterile bandage that could be instantly applied, what a lot of suffering it would save.

He had released a Golden Nugget of creative thought to his subconscious mind, without being aware of it. Within a few days he suddenly got an idea to create a simple, sterile bandage that could instantly be applied by even a child. In that moment was born the bandage known as a Band-Aid and its creator, Robert W. Johnson went on to make a multimillion-dollar-a-year business out of the Golden Nugget that he had fed into his subconscious mind!

## POINTS TO REMEMBER

1. The power to change your creative thinking into solid golden nuggets that can bring you money, fame, power, or anything else that you desire is yours.
2. The goose that lays the golden eggs releases a Golden Nugget a day from your subconscious mind for money, your own business, or building some great creative talent.
3. A young woman released the Golden Nuggets of her mind to bring her the sum of $15,000 that her dead father had hidden in a chest of drawers.
4. A woman who worked for a big manufacturing concern programmed that she would come into big money. She met a man on a plane who made her a district representative and she was soon making $15,000 a year from sales and commissions.

5. The Golden Nugget concept can show you how to make money through real estate, stocks and bonds or other investments.

6. A woman who used this subconscious mind programming asked for $100,000 or more through land investments. She bought property in the Grand Bahamas, Arizona and New Mexico and in a few years she realized that sum from her investments.

7. The golden nugget can help you develop a great creative talent to become an artist, writer, inventor, composer, a singer or actor or dancer, or anything else you choose as your talent.

8. A top Hollywood dress designer programmed that she would build a big income. She has had three Oscar nominations and is now in the $50,000-a-year income class.

9. Trigger instant subconscious Golden Nuggets to bring you money or jewels, clothing, TV sets, hi-fi sets, refrigerators or any other material object you desire.

10. A woman instantly obtained a $5,000 mink coat when she didn't have a penny in the bank.

11. You can trigger subconscious gold from the mental conditioner to enable you to help your family, educate your children and give them financial security for the future.

12. A man built a multimillion dollar a year business through this subconscious Golden Nugget and developed Band-Aids.

# *HOW TO BUILD THE MILLION-DOLLAR CONSCIOUSNESS FOR PERSONAL WEALTH*

# 3

You can magnetize your higher mind centers with the million-dollar consciousness and begin to instantly think, feel, look and live like a millionaire.

It is in the mental realm that you first must begin to think you are going to be a millionaire. In the realm of the mind all things are possible. Mental concepts have always preceded physical action and material achievement.

It was in his mind that man first visualized himself flying like a bird. Realization of this dream came after he had built the consciousness that he could fly.

In back of every great fortune there is the million dollar consciousness first. Every person who became a millionaire first had to think in terms of big money and success. A limited consciousness brings a limited income. When you expand your mind and visualize new money horizons, you will soon be thinking like a successful and rich person.

In this chapter we shall study the techniques for building the million-dollar consciousness, so that you can begin instantly to think, talk, look and act like you already have the million dollar fortune you are projecting.

## REGIMEN TO BUILD
## THE MILLION-DOLLAR CONSCIOUSNESS

1. **To imprint the idea of infinite riches on your higher consciousness, take the Millionaire's Secret Vow of Riches.**

Every person who achieves a big fortune has made a secret pact with his higher, subconscious mind. Sometimes it is no more than just a mental determination to be rich and successful. Sometimes it is more clearly and deliberately stated in written or spoken form and becomes a dynamic command to the subconscious mind to build a fortune.

## THE MILLIONAIRE'S SECRET VOW OF RICHES

Repeat the following Secret Vow of Riches every day for the next month, until it becomes so firmly engraved on your subconscious mind that it is an automatic part of your mental and physical reflex action.

> I now take the Millionaire's Vow for Riches. I recognize that there are infinite treasures in the Cosmic Cornucopia of Riches and Abundance. I draw upon the unlimited resources of the universe for my own enrichment.
> I desire unlimited supplies of money and material goods so that I may use my riches to help my family and to give something of value to the world.
> I recognize that I am only a channel for the release of God's treasures for the enrichment of the world. I therefore vow that I shall do only good with my future fortune.
> I take an oath that I shall use money to help uplift those who

are downtrodden; to liberate those imprisoned by poverty; to idealize the standards of the world; to strive to help children, the sick, the poor, the imprisoned, the blind and crippled, so they may know greater joy.

I shall use my money and earthly treasures to educate, inspire and uplift humanity; to help bring peace to the world, to banish discrimination and racial prejudice; to bring about equality for all; and to use my supply and abundance for the good of humanity and the greater glory of God.

When you once involve the thought of riches in your subconscious mind it begins to evolve the methods for you to achieve the fortune you desire.

A man who married when he was 24 was so poor that he didn't have the money to buy an engagement ring. On the day of his wedding he gave his wife a check made out for a date 25 years from that day for $25,000. He told his wife to cash the check on that future date.

Both of them forgot this beautiful wedding gift from a loving but poor husband, but the man's subconscious mind did not forget this vow of riches that was prompted by his loving heart. Exactly 25 years later this man was a millionaire, and one day his wife ran across the check and on their twenty-fifth wedding anniversary she cashed it without question or doubt that it would be good!

Such is the power of your higher mind when you program it with the million-dollar consciousness; it will set about automatically to bring you everything you involve in your higher mind centers.

Another interesting example of how the subconscious mind never forgets a vow of riches when it is sincerely made was that of another man who married a girl, with no future prospects that he would ever be rich. However, he vowed to her on their wedding day that on their tenth wedding anniversary he would present her with a special gift—a $10,000 string of real pearls. This man became a big business success in that period of time and right on schedule, he gave his wife a beautiful pearl necklace worth $10,000!

2. **Create your own Golden Hall of Fame, where you join the invisible brotherhood of rich, famous and influential people.**

To do this you obtain a scrapbook, the type you put snapshots in. Then cut out of magazines and newspapers the pictures and names of people who are rich, famous, successful, or gifted in some special way.

This Golden Hall of Fame can include movie stars, TV personalities, political figures, millionaires in industry, inventors, composers, great lawyers, doctors, explorers, writers, artists, space astronauts, sports stars, scientists, educators, religious leaders—in fact, any person you admire or that you wish to emulate and pattern your success after.

A few of these famous people you might want to add to your Golden Hall of Fame might be Onassis, Rockefeller, Howard Hughes, J. Paul Getty, Bing Crosby, W. Clement Stone, Churchill, the late President Roosevelt, Richard Nixon, or any other person you admire. If you do not have a photograph from a magazine or newspaper, just write down the person's name on the page. Then put your photograph on the same page with these famous and successful people.

Each night, just before going to bed, look at yourself in the Golden Hall of Fame with these illustrious persons and give yourself the following subconscious programming for riches.

> I now elevate myself to the Golden Hall of Fame with the immortals, the rich, the successful, and I program my subconscious mind to make me worthy of a place alongside these illustrious persons.
>
> I ask for the talents and the riches and recognition that these people have earned, and promise myself that I shall strive

to be worthy of the high goals and the riches that I ask for. I have confidence in my ability to rise to high places, and I now accept the glory and recognition that shall be mine.

3. Take an inventory of your present treasures; realize that you may already be enjoying some things that all millionaires do not now have.

You cannot always equate money with happiness. You may have the health, happiness and peace of mind that is often denied to those who have millions. It is always good to take a mental inventory of your present riches and to realize that you may already have treasures that money in itself cannot buy.

In the past few years five multimillionaires committed suicide! They had everything money could buy but they were so miserable they could not face life. You can have millions and still be happy, but without millions, you should not be miserable. If you correctly inventory your present treasures you will find you may have more than many millionaires.

The Million-Dollar Inventory Should Include:

A. Peace of mind.

B. Good friends who like you for yourself, not your money.

C. Good health, mentally and physically, without pain or anxiety about the future.

D. Love, happiness, marriage, a family of your own. These are treasures money cannot buy.

E. Creative work that you enjoy and which you do not do just for money, but for satisfaction.

F. Peace of soul with faith in God and spiritual security, which gives you the treasures of spirit, are often denied to those who make money their God.

To show you how millions of dollars do not always buy happiness, I once was in a barber shop when a very rich man came in to have his hair cut. It was obvious he was a very rich man by the way everyone bustled to wait on him. The manicurist rushed to his side; the shoe-shine boy began to polish his shoes; the barber practically bowed as he began to give him a haircut and shave.

The man had a big diamond stickpin in his tie, which was in the shape of a horseshoe. He wore a huge diamond ring on his finger. His clothes were tailor-made and obviously expensive. He was, one could see at a glance, a big shot.

When this man left the barber shop he gave everyone a generous tip and my barber turned to me and said, "Do you know who that man was?"

I said, "No, who was he?"

He replied, "That's one of the big racketeers in this city. He owns race horses, has beer trucks, numbers rackets, and everything you could name that is illegal. He's worth millions of dollars."

Then he went on to tell me that the man suffered from high blood pressure, had recently had two severe heart attacks, his wife had just run off with a younger man, and his six-year-old son had just been run over by a truck—yes, you guessed it, by a beer truck! The barber went on to say, "That man's money can buy him everything but love, peace of mind, health, happiness, and his son's life."

I wanted to also add, "His money can buy him everything but heaven!"

Yes, you can have a million dollars and still be happy. But if you make money your God, you will probably lose out on the true spiritual, mental and moral treasures of life

4. **Protect your image of the wealth you will one day have by** *now* **taking a mental inventory of the things you want money for in the future.**

Your subconscious mind will be deeply impressed by such a survey of the riches you hope to have and the things you wish to do with your money. You can call this projection of future wealth.

## YOUR MONEY BLUEPRINT FOR THE FUTURE

Under this heading list the things you want money for, and the sums of money you feel you need for future security. Your list might look like the following, or you can make up one to suit your exact needs.

A. I would like work in which I shall be able to make $15,000 a year to meet my future needs.

B. I would like to be in my own business making $50,000 or more a year. (Here, try to be specific telling your subconscious mind if you want a restaurant, a beauty shop, a health food store, a machine shop, a garage, an interior decorating business, a photographic studio; or some kind of business where you give service to the public such as accounting, repairing machines, income tax returns, health services, or any other special type of service.)

C. I would like to buy a new car of the following make, model and color. (Here describe the type of car you desire and the approximate cost. Do not be ashamed to buy a second-hand car if your pocketbook is not overflowing with money at present, for this is a beginning, and later it can be turned in on a new car.)

I know a very wealthy man and his wife who could afford to buy a new car every year, but for 25 years, he told me, he has bought a second-hand Cadillac with about 50,000 miles on it. He was told by a good mechanic that a Cadillac is just about broken in at that time and is a much better buy than a new car. He keeps the car an average of five years and then turns it in on another one, thus keeping up on modern mechanical improvements.

D. I want to buy a home of my own, in which to bring up

my family and give them confort and security. I want the house
to be located in the country. (Here it is important to state the
location you want, the style of architecture, the number of
rooms and other details about its furnishings.) It is also
important to pick the class of house you want; if it is to be a
small cottage, obviously your money requirements will be more
reasonable than if it is to be a mansion. It is important that you
let your subconscious mind know what you expect, for it must
prepare itself to reveal the methods by which you can make the
larger sums to pay for the bigger house.

For example: A man and his wife in California came into
our work and learned about Subconscious Money Programming.
They were married and had two children when I met them, but
the man was working for a salary in a leather goods store, where
he was a salesman and made good commissions. However, they
could never look forward to big sums of money nor a big house.

This man had been reared in Texas and his father had a
leather goods shop, where he manufactured hand-made wallets,
handbags for women, make-up kits, and even fancy cowboy
boots for rodeo stars.

When he told me his big ambitions, I quoted the Bible, and
asked, "What hast thou in thine house?"

He replied, "I am good in making leather objects." Then he
showed me a hand-made, leather wallet made of ostrich skin,
which he had created. It cost him only the price of the leather
and it was easily worth $150 on the market.

He said, "But I don't have the money to open a shop."

He then told me he had a leather sewing machine in his
home, so I told him, "Why don't you begin with what you now
have and take orders for wallets, boots, and handbags from your
friends, and do the work in your spare time in your own
apartment?"

He had not thought of that, but he decided he would begin
the following week. He had cards made up, telling of his

specialty in hand-made leather goods, and featuring a pair of cowboy boots, in color, on the front of his card.

He later told me the astounding story of how his subconscious mind shaped his entire money-making desires into a practical idea to instantly bring him a bigger income.

A friend of his, for whom he made a pocketbook for free, received one of his cards. He worked in studios as a carpenter, and it just happened that he had met one of the big cowboy stars at that particular studio. This man was always buying new boots, holsters, saddles, and other leather goods for his work. One day he called up this leather-worker and ordered a half-dozen pair of boots, a new holster, and other equipment, including a suede jacket for his wife. The upshot of this was that the movie star was so impressed by this man's work that he offered to back him in his own shop, and told him he could pay the money back as he earned it! If he lost, he could take it off his taxes!

With this big loan, the man from Texas opened a small leather business, hired three assistants, and with his connection with studios already formed, other cowboy stars, recording artists and the general public began to patronize his business.

Now, exactly three years later, this man has one of the most successful leather goods manufacturing businesses on the West Coast. He repaid the movie star's loan, put a big down payment on his dream home out in San Fernando Valley, and is on his way to making his first million dollars!

E. I want the sum of $100,000 for future overall security, so I may have the leisure to travel, to advance my cultural interests, and to give my children a higher education.

This general, overall statement can include specific things you want in your life that will require large sums of money. If you know these things and write them down on your Future Money Inventory, they will be caught up in the automatic processes of your computerlike subconscious mind and be more likely to evolve. If you do not have any such specific goals or sums of money in mind, you will never receive subconscious guidance to the achievement of your higher money goals.

A woman in California used this method to program into her subconscious mind that she wanted the sum of $1,000 for a specific immediate need. She had two children, a boy of 17 and a girl of 19. She wanted them to have a trip to Hawaii during their summer vacation. She and her husband had been to Hawaii on their honeymoon and she wanted her children to share in that wonderful trip, so they would have beautiful memories for the future.

Within one month her husband received a $2,000 bonus for a big deal he had put over for his firm, and the entire family went to Hawaii on their vacation. If this woman and her husband had not projected these extra sums of money, he might not have had the inspiration to put over the big deal! Very often it takes such an emotional motivating desire to prod the subconscious mind to make that extra effort which can bring additional sums of money for specific purposes.

F. Carry at all times in your pocketbook a check made out to yourself for $1,000,000. Sign the check, God, the Universal Banker. Look at the check at least three times a day and begin to imprint on your subconscious mind the following programming:

I now posess a million dollars or more in cashable assets. The resources of the universe are mine, as well as anyone else's. The gold, silver, oil, iron, uranium and all the products of earth, including agricultural ones, are mine. I possess the free parks, the museums, art galleries, public libraries and theaters. I own the subway and bus and other transportation. I possess the millions of dollars worth of entertainment on radio and television which I may have every day of my life. I now claim my divine inheritance and realize that now, in this moment, I have more than a million dollars in assets, which I may use and enjoy freely.

G. Form a Treasure Chest in which you magnetize the elements you desire in jewels, stocks, deeds to property, or other riches you want your subconscious mind to program for your future.

For this purpose obtain a small box, such as a man uses as a cufflink box, or a lady uses for a jewel box. Label this box MY TREASURE CHEST. Then put in the following items (if you do not have the real article, an imitation will do): A small piece of gold or silver and a bag of colored glass to simulate a diamond, pearl, ruby, emerald or other precious stone. Write down on small sheets of paper, THE DEED TO MY DREAM HOME. On another sheet write 1,000 shares of General Motors, or some other stock that you will find listed in the financial pages of the newspapers. Then take 10 pieces of paper and cut them the size and shape of money, and put in the four corners of each piece the sum of $10,000. These 10 sheets now number up to $100,000. You can count these over each night before going to bed, visualizing them as being real money, and daydreaming on how you will spend this money.

If you wish to build the million-dollar consciousness you can use the Treasure Chest principle by cutting out 10 sheets of paper and numbering them in the four corners with the figure of $100,000. These 10 sheets now add up to $1,000,000.

To treat your subconscious mind to a perpetual money feast, make it a point to look at your treasures each day at least once, preferably just before going to bed at night. Your subconscious mind will be deeply impressed by these objects, and you will be magnetizing your brain centers to respond with money-making ideas that will soon start the flow of money, goods and precious gifts into your life.

A young lady who used this method to bring her money or its equivalents had always wanted a big diamond ring. She was engaged at the time she learned about this method of subconscious mind programming, but her fiance did not have the money to buy her a big engagement ring. She began her

Treasure Chest and put into it the dream home for the future, and a piece of glass which she mentally labeled as a diamond.

Within one week, her future mother-in-law called her on the telephone and told her she wanted to see her. When the girl arrived at her home the woman took out a small jewel case and said, "I don't know why, but yesterday something made me go to my safety deposit box at the bank and take out this jewel which my husband gave me 30 years ago. When he died I put it in the vault and have never worn it since."

The woman opened the little jewel box and there was a magnificent big blue-white diamond ring! She said, "Here, I want you to have it."

Later, this same girl, after she had married, received as gifts from her mother-in-law a string of real pearls, a ruby ring, a diamond and sapphire pin, and other trinkets that were given to her as gifts! Her subconscious mind somehow sent out the cosmic command to the only source from which she could receive these treasures she had mentally programmed!

H. Create your Scrapbook of Destiny to build a million-dollar consciousness. Take an ordinary scrapbook and paste into it all newspaper or magazine pictures of houses, cars, furs, furnishings, or other objects you want to attract.

Besides actual pictures of objects, you may also put into your scrapbook any articles dealing with the lives of wealthy persons, their methods for building their fortunes, and items from the financial pages of newspapers about the stock market or big business. Let these financial items furnish your subconscious mind with the consciousness of big money and methods that wealthy and successful people have used to build their personal fortunes.

Whenever you want to build a bigger money consciousness glance through your Money Scrapbook and read the various stories of how millionaires have built their fortunes. Then let the information sink into your subconscious mind. Later you will be automatically guided to take steps that cause you to attract money or get big business ideas that can make you rich.

## POINTS TO REMEMBER

1. You can magnetize your brain centers and begin to think, look and act like a millionaire, giving you benefits of riches even before you have a million.
2. The Millionaire's Secret Vow of Riches can instantly put you into the millionaire class and build the consciousness of unlimited wealth.
3. A young man who took this vow of wealth was able to give his wife a check for $25,000 to cash 25 years later. By that time his subconscious mind had made him rich.
4. Put yourself into the Millionaire's Golden Hall of Fame, and begin at once to feel like a millionaire.
5. Take a mental inventory of your present riches, and begin to enjoy these treasures which many millionaires do not possess.
6. Your million-dollar inventory should include friends, good health, love, happiness, creative work, mental peace and spiritual serenity.
7. A man who was rich but not happy had everything money could buy except love, health, happiness, peace of mind and soul serenity.
8. Build your Money Blueprint for the future, and program your subconscious mind with big money ideas, a business of your own, a beautiful car, your dream home, and money with which you can travel, afford luxuries and educate your future children.
9. A man who wanted to be in his own business used the Bible injunction, "What hast thou in thine house?" to program his subconscious mind into a big leather goods business that made him rich within three years.

10. One woman programmed a trip to Hawaii for her vacation, and her husband received a bonus of $2,000 which made this possible.

11. Program your subconscious mind by carrying a check made out to yourself for $1,000,000 and by building money awareness.

12. Use the Treasure Chest to plant in your subconscious mind gifts of jewels, a home of your own, and other precious objects.

13. Start the perpetual flow of money by cutting out pieces of paper and labeling them $10,000 each, until you have built a consciousness of from $100,000 to $1,000,000.

14. One young lady wanted a big diamond engagement ring, but her boy friend could not afford it. She got the big ring within one week from the time she programmed her subconscious.

15. Build your Money Scrapbook of Destiny to chart your destiny for attracting houses, lands, cars, jewels, stocks and other things of value that you desire.

# READ THE SIGNPOSTS ON THE ROYAL ROAD TO RICHES

# 4

There is a royal road to riches that you may discover and it will lead you to unlimited supplies of money and the things that money can buy. This royal road to riches is marked by certain signposts that can accurately guide you to the achievement of fame and fortune. When you follow these signposts, which other rich people have observed, you will ultimately reach your goal in life and achieve success and unlimited riches.

In this chapter we shall explore some of these signposts that lead you to the royal road to riches and discover how you may avoid the pitfalls that often keep people from achieving success and abundance.

### Signpost No. 1: A desire for a big fortune

Write down on a file card this signpost for riches and the things you desire in your life. Then list the most prominent things you would like to do with your money.

A. I desire money so I may give my family security.
B. I desire a fortune so I may travel and have more leisure to pursue artistic and intellectual activities.
C. I desire $100,000 to educate my children.

D. I desire large sums of money so I may have my own home, a beautiful car, and the luxuries and comforts that make life pleasurable.

E. I desire a big business success and a fortune so I may endow charitable institutions, help orphans, veterans, establish peace, and bring about better racial relations.

F. I desire a million dollars so I may create a foundation that will do scientific research in medicine and health to bring longer life and better health to the world.

G. I wish to become famous, rich and powerful for personal satisfaction and joy of accomplishment.

You may select any of these seven desires for building a fortune, or you may choose all of them to give you the impetus towards success, fame and riches.

Obviously the desires listed under A, B, C, and D are the most common ones that motivate millions of people. You should choose the particular desires that fit your needs and then write them down on file cards which you can keep in a place where you are reminded daily of these motivating forces.

A man I once knew, who used this method, had the desire to give his family security, but at the same time he wanted money so he could give his children a college education, and then, later in life, he wanted to be able to travel and enjoy cultural benefits which his money could buy.

Obviously, all these things did not come to him in a year or two. The first thing that did come was his own business, which gave him financial security. Then, gradually over a period of five years, he had an income that gave him the future security he asked for, as well as enough to educate his three children in later years.

**Signpost No. 2: A creative imagination and ability to use the powers of visualization**

Most of the great things created in this age of miracles have come about because of this signpost on the royal road to riches. Man's creative imagination has been responsible for TV, automobiles, air conditioning, telephones, motion pictures, airplanes and space ships, computers, electric power, and the millions of amazing inventions that have blessed this age.

## THE THREE ASPECTS OF IMAGINATION YOU CAN USE

**A. Concentration.** To utilize the creative power of your imagination it is necessary that you sit each day and concentrate your creative power in a positive, direct manner on the things you wish to do in the future.

Concentrate for five minutes on your work and see in your imagination how you might change it to be more productive.

Concentrate another five minutes on your money matters; are you utilizing money correctly to get the greatest yield on your investments? Could you put your money into something other than a savings account which might yield a greater income?

Concentrate on releasing the power of your imagination on new ideas that might prove helpful in bringing you money. Visualize yourself in another job, or in a business of your own. See yourself creating something or inventing an object that could bring you a fortune.

**B. Emotional Intensification.** An ordinary use of the imagination is not as effective as emotional intensification. Almost everyone thinks occasionally, "I'd like to have a million dollars so I could do the things I want to do." But this is not an original or intense use of imaginative power. You must want something so intensely that you charge your brain centers with the magnetic quality of attraction and it will then come to you.

A woman I once knew in California was left by her husband with two small children to rear. She had no work, no money and seemingly no way to get out of her difficulties.

When she came to me for my advice on her problems, I asked her what work she could best do. She replied, "I have always been good at working with my hands in needlework, knitting, and making curtains for friends and relatives. But how could I do this, when I have never had any professional training?"

I told her to program her subconscious mind with the following positive statement and to then await results from her higher mind. She was to repeat three times a day the following mental programmers:

> I am a channel for higher mind to work through me. My subconscious knows my talents. I now ask guidance as to how I can convert these gifts into money or its equivalents. I desire money to help give security to my two children, and to own a home of my own in the future. I now confidently await guidance on the next steps I shall take to bring me in a steady income.

This woman reported to me only two weeks later and was so excited she could hardly tell me what had happened.

A woman, for whom she had graciously made a set of beautiful window drapes for free, knew a wealthy woman who had a beautiful new home she was furnishing. She needed drapes for her entire house and she was willing to order them from this talented woman who had been using her gifts for the good of her friends and relatives.

Through a friend, who was a credited interior decorator, she was able to order her materials from a wholesale house at a very good discount, and she enlisted the aid of two other seamstresses to help her with the big job she had undertaken. The outcome of this first venture in her own business was that the wealthy woman was delighted with the beautiful work she did, and recommended her to friends in the Beverly Hills and Bel-Air set. She had cards printed and distributed and soon her phone was ringing all day with orders for bedspreads, curtains, and other homemaking objects which she created.

Money began pouring in, but the big thing that happened came a year later. She hired a staff of three smart women and equipped them with kits of materials showing her products and photographs of work she had already done. These three women solicited new homes, worked with decorating firms, and received orders for complete drapery and upholstery services. The new venture was an instant success and soon this woman rented a big loft and had a staff of 10 people turning out her magnificent wares! She is now living in a magnificent home in Beverly Hills, and has her manager and her staff who do the actual selling and work, while she banks the money and rides in a beautiful new Cadillac!

You have some special gift; probe your imagination and concentrate your mind power on discovering what it is. If you have no such special gift ask your subconscious mind to direct you to something that you can do and see how quickly you will be on the royal road to riches!

**C. Imagination without action seldom produces a fortune.** The third aspect of imagination is projection.

You must begin to project the visual images you have to the outer world of reality and take that first step to bring it into reality. Your creative power works very much like a motion picture projector, which is loaded with film on which there are inscribed pictures or images. When light shines through the projector those images are projected to the outer screen and take on form and reality.

Your brain is the projector; your thoughts are the film, and the pictures on that film have been placed there by your images that you have created within your imagination. If these images are weak and indefinite, they will project to the outer world indecision, lack, limitation and failure. If you make these images strong through emotional intensification and project your images to the outer world, they will soon take shape and bring you the success and riches you desire.

If you want to write a great novel, hold the mental image first; then intensify it emotionally by having a great desire to entertain the world and enrich yourself. Then take the first step to externalize this image; buy a typewriter, learn how to use it, get a piece of paper and insert it in the typewriter and then ask your subconscious mind for ideas to write that first novel.

I know a young man of 26 who did exactly this. He had been in prison in the South and was released. He came to New York City and wandered into one of my lectures where he learned how he could change his entire life through subconscious programming.

He asked himself what gift he had; he found he had none. But suddenly his subconscious reminded him of the brutal prison experiences he had known. He sat down and wrote down his recollections, weaving them into a story; he could not even type but a friend rewrote the manuscript on a typewriter. They sent it to an agent and the first novel was published but sold only 1,000 copies. However, a motion picture company saw the novel and offered him $85,000 for the picture rights!

From that mental projection this young writer went on to other successes. He was hired at a big salary to write the film version and since that time has done other novels.

**Signpost No. 3:** Use the 24 golden hours of each day wisely

This signpost can definitely put your feet on the royal road to riches.

Most people waste several hours a day on usual pursuits and never have the necessary time to concentrate their mind power on becoming wealthy.

You only have 24 hours a day to spend. Eight hours are

required for sleep and relaxation. Eight hours you work, and only eight hours a day are left for you to spend as you wish.

If you spend two hours each day looking at television or in other forms of entertainment, you still have six precious hours left. Let us say that preparing food and eating take up three hours—then you have only three hours out of 24 left to devote to self-improvement or to studying methods for building a fortune.

Most people never find this royal road to riches because they waste the precious gold of life on useless pursuits. If you spend only three hours a day on concentrating your mind power on how you can make a fortune, you will soon be able to discover the means for going into a new business, discovering a new object that could make you a fortune, or perfecting some talent that could bring you a million dollars in the future.

A woman came to me once at one of my lectures and complained, "After I do my housework and take care of my two growing children, I have no time to develop creative talents. What can I do?"

I then told her a story about a nurse who had three children. Her husband was gone and she was forced to work 12 hours a day in a hospital to make money to support her children. She chose night work. She had a terrific desire to make a fortune so she could give her children future security. She decided she would become a writer. She learned everything she could about writing novels. Then, despite the fact she worked 12 hours each night, she would return to her home, prepare breakfast for her three children, pack their lunches and send them off to school. Then she would sit at her desk and write until she dropped off to sleep from sheer exhaustion.

This courageous woman finished her novel, sent it off to a publisher and awaited results. Her novel was accepted and she began writing other novels, still working nights at her profession of nursing. The novelist became famous and earned $5,000,000 at her writing and from movie rights. Her name was Mary Roberts Rhinehart.

When I finished this story this woman replied, "I get the point. If I want something badly enough I'll find the time to get it."

This woman later studied art, and although she did not have a great talent, she found an outlet for her gifts. She began doing photo coloring in her spare time at home, and the big photographers sent her large photos which she colored. In this way she often made as much as $100 a week extra.

To wisely utilize the golden hours of each day, you must have a definite schedule to follow. This should include the daily use of your spare hours, so you utilize them wisely and profitably.

Your schedule might look like this:

**Monday.** Today I shall learn three new words that I can use in my writing and conversation which will help me expand my mind in a positive manner.

**Tuesday.** Today I shall contact four people by telephone or letter on some new business idea, or for sales possibilities of my product. (Or it might be an interview with a company that you want to work with.)

**Wednesday.** This day I shall study the life of some important and wealthy person and learn his business secrets and emulate the pattern of his thinking in my own effort to become rich.

**Thursday.** I shall sit for half an hour today trying to receive some guidance from my subconscious mind on some way to improve my life, to better my work, or to receive an idea for an invention or an improvement of some product I use every day.

**Friday.** This day I shall study the business section of the daily paper, learning of people who have made fortunes through the stock market or through business methods they have used.

(This can be such magazines as *Fortune, Forbes,* or other financial publications.)

**Saturday.** Today I shall write two letters to future prospects who might be able to help me merchandise my product, or use my services in their business.

**Sunday.** Today I shall give thanks to God for my blessings and appraise all my true riches: peace of mind, love, happiness, good mental and physical health, true friends, my family, and my gifts and talents which are God-given. I shall this day realize that I am abundantly blessed with a million dollars worth of riches that money cannot buy.

### Signpost No. 4: Build positive mental habits

Making money can become a habit, just like anything else. Big money-makers have learned to build a positive mental attitude and to create positive habit patterns regarding money.

To build this positive mental habit, start being conscious of every dollar you earn and spend. Make a brief record each day of money spent and then total it at the end of each week to imprint on your mind what you are doing with your money. The saying, "Take care of the pennies and the dollars will take care of themselves" is based on this mental habit of money awareness.

The first John D. Rockefeller kept a diary when he was a young boy. In it he listed his daily expenses. One such item says, "Two cents put into the collection plate this Sunday." A mind that built such positive money habits when young could not help but become a big financial success.

Also in this money diary you might list sums of money earned, money that comes to you from unexpected sources, and money you hope to gain for meeting future needs.

### Signpost No. 5: Be enthusiastic about the product you have to sell or the services you have to offer the public

One of the secret ingredients in back of every big fortune that has ever been built is enthusiasm. If you do not have enthusiasm regarding your present job, give it up and get into something you love to do.

Enthusiasm creates mental and physical energy. You can be enthusiastic about making money, it is true, but you must have something you enjoy doing before money will begin to pour into your bank account.

A man named Dean Arnold was enthusiastic about baking products that would help the American housewife serve her family good, nourishing bread. He started with the National Biscuit Company in the early 1930s, during the depression. Later he lost that job and decided to branch out on his own. With only a $1,000 of his savings, he started his own bakeshop in Greenwich, Connecticut. His enthusiasm kept him striving to perfect his baked goods until 1943 when he began to really make big money. Now Arnold Bakers sell their products in 28 states or more, and he is the head of a $10-million-dollar-a-year business, which is still expanding.

What special gift or talent do you have? Are you enthusiastic about your product or talent? Do you show this enthusiasm when you talk to others? When you are truly enthusiastic it is like a contagion that soon spreads to others, making them eager to help you grow rich.

Another man became enthusiastic about ice cream. There are many ice cream companies but this man believed that he had one of the finest products in the world. He opened a small business in a suburban town and began to sell his product. Soon he was franchising his soft ice cream to operators throughout the country. He developed Dari-Freeze ice cream, which was sold by distributors who paid him a royalty on every gallon sold. Soon Tom Carvel was selling freezers and franchises for his different ice cream and collecting royalties from all his dealers throughout the country.

The Carvel chain of stores now grosses more than $3 million a year and is still growing. The signpost on his royal road to riches was clearly marked. It was *enthusiasm.*

### Signpost No. 6: Perseverance and persistence

One of the earmarks of a rich, successful person is the fact that he is persevering and persistent.

Most people try something a few times and then give up in defeat. Hardly any of the 10,000 rich people whose lives I have studied to learn their secrets of magnetizing money ever made it in one try. They often had to persevere for a period of several years before they struck it rich.

The man who first developed ball-point pens in 1946 had a good idea, but his pens were too expensive. Another man came along, who persevered with his idea that he could produce a ball-point pen that would sell for $1.69. This man's name was Patrick Frawley and he perfected Paper-Mate, which was soon one of the fastest selling pens in the business. He persisted with his attempts to find a perfect, fast-drying ink for his pens. Frawley did—and is making millions of pens a year at a terrific profit.

Whatever ideas you receive from your subconscious mind for building your own personal fortune, never give up until you have explored every possible avenue for achieving success.

If you find you have made the wrong choice of a product or the service you are giving is not adequate to build a fortune, do not become discouraged and feel you have failed. Try another product or service and then keep on until you have broken through the barrier to success. Almost all great fortunes were built only after trying several different ways for achieving a fortune. When the right formula is discovered never let your mind waver from your determination to become rich through your product or your services.

## POINTS TO REMEMBER

1. You can discover the royal road to riches that will lead you to unlimited wealth by probing within your own mind and searching for the signposts that are placed on the pathway to fame and fortune.

2. Signpost No. 1: A desire for a big fortune. How you may intensify your desires with the list of the most prominent things you would like to do with your money when you get it.

3. Signpost No. 2: A creative imagination and the ability to use your powers of visualization. Learn how to use your imagination to forge success and riches in your life.

4. A woman with two children created her success by using her imagination and her special creative gift of sewing.

5. A young man used his imagination to write a novel that later sold to movies for $85,000.

6. Signpost No. 3: Use the 24 golden hours a day you have wisely. This signpost will lead you to find the golden road to riches and success.

7. One woman, who had three children, used her time constructively and earned $5,000,000 through her movies and novels.

8. Make out a time schedule to magnetize money, and utilize the golden hours of each day in a positive manner.

9. Signpost No. 4: Build positive mental habits in regard to making and spending money. John D. Rockefeller kept a money diary showing his expenses even as a child.

10. Signpost No. 5: Be enthusiastic about your product or the services you have to sell and it will magnetize your brain centers to build a big fortune.

11. One man was enthusiastic about baking bread and built a multimillion dollar fortune.

12. Signpost No. 6: Have perseverance and persistence if you wish to build a fortune. One man who was persistent perfected the ball-point pen known as Paper-Mate and is now making millions of pens and a fortune every year.

# PROJECT MONEY MAGNETISM
## TO INFLUENCE AND CONTROL
## WEALTHY PEOPLE

# 5

One of the quickest ways for you to build money magnetism is to associate with people who have already used the power of magnetism to become rich. In your community there are people who have proved successful in their own fields. These people have used tried and tested formulas for achieving their success. You can profit by listening to their advice and following their suggestions. You can magnetize their minds with your own projections of thoughts that will endear them to you and make them want to help you.

In this chapter we shall examine some of the ways by which you can project money magnetism to rich people and cause them to help you achieve your money goals in life.

## 10 WAYS TO MEET
## WEALTHY AND PROMINENT PEOPLE

1. One of the easiest ways for you to meet wealthy and important people is to go where such people congregate. It is

almost impossible to casually run into such people, but they do go to certain places where you can accidentally cross their paths.

Choose a church where there are regular social events scheduled for the parishioners and attend it every week until you become a regular part of the scene. Then when there are social events, charitable, money-raising bazaars, or other church functions, you will automatically become a part of the scene. In this way you will meet and mingle with outstanding citizens of your community. Soon you will be invited to the homes of prominent people and such contacts will eventually lead to some kind of business or financial involvement.

A young man and his wife came to our lectures in Los Angeles, and they were eager to move into higher circles socially and for business reasons. The young man was a beginning attorney and they were anxious to start building their lives on a solid social foundation.

They followed my advice to join a church of their faith in the wealthy Beverly Hills district. Soon they were making contacts with other church members, some of whom were very important in the business community. One of these contacts was with a judge and his wife. They found the young couple charming and invited them to a small dinner party at their home. It was at this party that the young attorney met a man who was prominent in city government. Later when he needed an assistant in his office, he just naturally chose the young attorney he had met socially! From this beginning this young attorney went on to become an outstanding lawyer, and later ran successfully for public office, backed by the judge and his former employer. He won out over his competition by a wide margin. This was the beginning of a great career for this young man and his wife.

2. One of the easiest places for you to meet wealthy and important people is through a social club. This can be an

Athletic club, a golf or tennis club, or a country club, where socially prominent people gather regularly. It may cost a little to join such a social club but when you once gain acceptance among such people, you will have many invitations and business contacts that will more than repay you for your investment.

A young real estate salesmen took my advice once to join the Beverly Hills Hotel Swimming Club. For a small yearly sum he and his wife had a poolside cabana, where they could meet with and entertain their friends all summer. Some of the people they met at the pool were wealthy people who were coming to California to live and they were in the market for houses or apartments.

Soon this real estate salesman was making more sales than anyone in his office. Within two years he opened his own real estate office in Beverly Hills and had 10 salesmen working for him. He was soon making friends among prominent businessmen and socialites, and his business operation became enormously successful, giving him security and prominence in his community.

3. To gain admittance to the offices of prominent and wealthy businessmen, write letters to 10 of the outstanding businessmen in your community, offering them ideas and suggestions for their business. Place no price tag on such ideas, but give them freely. If they are good ideas you will be given an interview and an opportunity of presenting them in person. After you have made these contacts you can later write letters to them asking if there are any openings in their organizations for your particular talents.

A young man just out of college wanted to get into advertising, but he had no contacts in that field. He learned these techniques for meeting important people by attending some of my lectures in New York City. He prepared an elaborate scrapbook in which he mounted all the important advertisements appearing in current periodicals and newspapers for cigarettes, cosmetics, household appliances, television sets, automobiles, food products and liquor ads. Then on each page he added his suggestions of how these ads could be improved so as to sell more products.

One particular firm that he approached happened to handle one of the products he had put into his scrapbook. It was a drug product. The advertising company used his suggestion for a television commercial, which instantly doubled the sale of the product! From that beginning this young man was given a job with one of the biggest advertising agencies in the city and a bonus of $10,000 for his new idea for a TV commercial!

4. To get into the higher brackets of social or business activities, make it a point to offer your services to any lodge or charitable group that is doing something for the good of the community or a particular charity, such as Lighthouse for the Blind, American Cancer Society, Multiple Sclerosis, Heart Fund, Jewish Charities, or any other group that has a standing in your community. You can participate in fund-raising campaigns, radio and television programs, house to house canvassing, or any other way in which you can be helpful.

Generally there are important people who are affiliated with these charitable groups. One sure way to meet these people is to be engaged in similar activities. Soon, you will be known to many of these people and when you need their aid or support, it will be simple for you to appeal to them for assistance in your career.

5. When you do meet important people who might help you in your career, show a sympathetic and understanding attitude towards them and their problems. As a rule most people think of highly placed people as being isolated from human emotions in their Olympian positions. However, many such people are lonely and eager for someone to talk to.

The story is told of a man named James Adamson, who

was trying to get an order for $90,000 from the big business-
man, George Eastman. He was told when he entered the great
man's presence not to take more than five minutes of his time
and then leave immediately. When this man was admitted to
Eastman's office he instantly admired the beauty of the sur-
roundings and complimented him on his good taste in furnishing it so tastefully. Eastman then began to tell him about some
wooden chairs he had just bought and repainted, and he
extended an invitation to Adamson to have lunch with him at
his home to see the hand-painted chairs. At that luncheon
Eastman poured out his heart to Adamson on all kinds of
subjects and the two men became good friends. When the
$90,000 order was given, who do you think Eastman chose? Of
course, it was his new friend Adamson!

6. Another way by which you will meet wealthy and
prominent people is at the playgrounds they select for their
vacations. It is as easy for you to choose a spot for your
vacation where important people go as it is to select some
out-of-the-way spot. In the winter these wealthy people go to
such places as Palm Springs, near Los Angeles; Acapulco, in
Mexico, which is a favorite resort place for many prominent
people; Miami Beach, Palm Beach, and Saint Petersburg, in
Florida; Honolulu; cruises on the Caribbean; the Bahamas, the
West Indies, and the Virgin Islands.

In the summer of course, these wealthy persons go regularly to such world capitals as London, Paris, Rome and Athens.
You can often meet them on airplanes or boats and trains. If
you show yourself interested in them and project friendliness,
you will be invited by them to their homes when they return
from vacations.

A young man and his wife were on the way to Rome. On
the same plane there was a courteous gentleman who was from
the oil-rich kingdom of Libya. They struck up a conversation
and before they arrived in Rome they had been invited to spend

several weeks with him in Paris and at his villa in Switzerland—
all expenses paid! This led to a very good friendship that later
paid rich dividends for the young businessman, as he was in
insurance and the friendly Libyan gave him his future business
when he came to America.

7. Always give that little extra measure of personal
attention and service to any person who comes into your
business place. You may be a secretary or switchboard operator,
but if you are courteous and kind, you cannot help but attract
interest.

A young lady who wanted to be a writer once worked at
the Mount Sinai Hospital in New York City in the private
pavillion where wealthy patients were often admitted. One day
she waited on the noted writer Fannie Hurst, and she was so
courteous that Fannie Hurst stopped to chat with her whenever
she visited her sick friend, Jascha Heifitz, the famous violinist.
The girl who worked at the switchboard during the day and
studied writing at night wrote a letter to Fannie Hurst, asking
her advice as to her future career as a writer. The great writer
sent her a most encouraging letter which so inspired the girl
that she went on to become a noted writer in her own field as a
great novelist.

8. When you do meet people who are important and who
might help you in your career, do not come right out and ask
them to help you. You can influence such a person to volunteer
his help by showing an attitude of cooperation with him. Make
him want to help you by showing him you respect his judgment
and admire his achievements. It flatters any person when someone admires his accomplishments and it makes him more than
willing to assist such a person.

9. Avoid controversial topics of conversation with people
you have just met and who might be able to help you. Any
person who is important and successful has usually won the
right to having his own way. He does not like opposition; make

it easy to get along with you by agreeing with him in what he says. This is especially true if he asks your opinion on some special subject.

10. Ask the advice of an important person, if you want to make him feel closer to you. Start by saying, "There's something I'd like your advice about.... "

This shows you believe in the superior quality of his intellect and it flatters him to think you have turned to him for advice because you know his background and experience qualify him to give you such advice.

Many times an important or wealthy person will become interested in your career if you ask him which one of two courses open to you should be taken for success.

A man who was a vice president of a large corporation was asked by a young man who wanted to get into his corporation how he should go about getting started in his career. The vice president thought for a moment and then replied, "Now that you ask, I think there's a position as a salesman in our organization, and if you qualify, you can quickly be promoted to a junior executive position at a very good salary."

This young man did not ask for a job, but he strongly hinted, by asking for advice and the executive quickly offered him his help.

Make up your mind early in your career that no person ever built his future success alone. There always have been others who have gone before on the royal road to riches, and these generous souls have reached out a helping hand to those just beginning the long, upward climb on the ladder of success.

## THE FIVE RULES GOVERNING SUCCESS MAGNETISM

1. Make it a point to always think in terms of positive success. Use expressions such as: I can succeed. I will be rich. I am important. I image the things I desire in my life. I think in

terms of big money. I achieve great things because I think of great accomplishment.

2. When you are with successful and important people never talk against wealthy people, nor show envy or jealousy. Always make an effort to praise these people and admire their accomplishments. You will not only win their approval but by this attitude of agreement, you show that you are ready to wear the mantle of riches and success.

3. Each day build money magnetism by concentrating for at least 15 minutes on money and its equivalents. Look at your Scrapbook of Destiny, filled with pictures of the home, car, clothes, furnishings, jewels and other things you desire and mentally claim these treasures. Count your pieces of paper on which you have written $1,000, $5,000 or $10,000, in the four corners. Add these up to a million dollars and get used to thinking in terms of big money and big success.

4. Every time you walk by store windows that are filled with treasures, stop and mentally say to yourself: "I now claim these riches of the universe for my own. I desire all those objects which will add comfort and pleasure to my life."

Whenever you see a beautiful home, put your mental magnetism to work to create a similar home for you and your family. Repeat to yourself, "I will soon have a home as beautiful as this one. I now mentally live in this home and entertain my friends there, enjoying its comfort and security.

Every time you see the make of car you desire stop and send your subconscious mind a suggestion that you will one day be riding in the same type of car. You can flash the telecosmic message: "I now claim that beautiful car. I desire the same make and model, and now project this car into my future."

Whenever you walk through a park, mentally claim it as your own estate, "I now claim the free parks and gardens as my own. The beautiful trees, flowers and shrubs are my cosmic riches and I appreciate them and enjoy their beauty. I myself will one day be worthy of my own private estate."

5. Every day, in whatever field you are in, give that extra little measure of service that will make you stand out. As you build your success consciousness by giving generously, you will, in turn, be given rewards by others.

A young lady who came to our lectures in Hollywood, California, worked in a poodle shop, giving service to pet owners. She loved dogs and to every customer that came into the shop she showed as much concern and interest as if the pets they had were her own.

One day an elderly woman came in with her white French poodle. This young lady gave her extra special attention and chatted with the woman about her beautiful dog, truly admiring his fine appearance. She gave the dog a beautiful haircut and when the woman came to pick up her dog, she was very impressed by the girl's courtesy and attention.

This woman returned many times over the ensuing months, and several times she mentioned that she worried constantly about what would become of her beloved pet if the woman died. The girl told her not to worry, that if she left it in her will that a sum of money be set aside for the care of her dog, it would be carried out by the executor of the will.

A little over a year later this wealthy woman died, and when the will was read, it was found she had left the sum of $50,000 to this girl, with the provision that she keep her pet until he died, and she could then use the money in any way she wished!

## POINTS TO REMEMBER

1. You can begin to build money magnetism through associating with people of wealth and importance and making them want to help you become rich.
2. You can literally hitch your wagon to the star of riches

and success and begin your climb up the ladder of riches and fame through people who have already achieved their goals.

3. Go to places where wealthy people congregate; this can be to a church or other community center, where you may meet such people.

4. A young man and his wife used their social connections to meet important people in legal fields that later won him an important public office.

5. You can meet important people by joining a club where these people congregate. Enlist their aid and support in your rise to fame and fortune.

6. Gain access to successful and important people through writing letters offering business ideas and suggestions.

7. One young man in advertising received $10,000 bonus for a new advertising idea for a big company.

8. You can offer your services to some charitable group such as Cancer or Heart Fund to help raise money, and in turn, receive assistance from important people who belong to these groups.

9. One man, who turned to George Eastman and used one of our principles for achieving success, received an order for furniture for $90,000 from the noted philanthropist and industrialist.

10. Plan your vacation so it will be in places where rich and important people congregate.

11. A man and his wife chose Rome for their vacation and met a millionaire oil man from Libya, and from him they received a gift of an all-expenses-paid vacation to Switzerland.

12. By giving that little extra measure of personal attention you will be able to win influential friends who may be able to help you in your climb to success.

13. A young lady won the interest of Fannie Hurst by being courteous and attentive, and was inspired by the noted writer to be a success in her future work.

14. Avoid controversial topics in conversation when you meet people who are rich or important.

15. Ask favors of those in high places and you will win their attention and interest.

16. The five rules governing success magnetism: think positively; never show envy or jealousy of rich people; build money magnetism by concentrating 15 minutes a day on wealth; go window shopping mentally and claim the world's riches; give that extra little measure of service to those you work with.

17. A young women won the attention of a rich woman, who later left her $50,000 in her will.

# DISCOVER THE GOLD MINE
# WITHIN YOURSELF
# THAT CAN MAKE YOU RICH

# 6

Every person has within his own mind a valuable Hidden Vein of Pure Gold, which, when brought to the surface of consciousness, can bring him fame and riches.

To find this Hidden Vein of Gold it is often necessary to dig deep within the subconscious mind until the precious nuggets of golden ideas are brought to the surface of consciousness.

All knowledge about the world in which you live is stored in your subconscious mind. Here it is that all material from the outer world is fed into your consciousness by your conscious mind. It is then sorted and filed away in memory paths that are etched deep in the convolutions of the brain. When you wish to call up any special facts, you turn to your subconscious mind and it releases its information related to that subject into your conscious mind.

Have you ever forgotten a name? You wracked your conscious mind and could not remember it. Then you began to say the letters of the alphabet, and suddenly, when you came to the right letter, the name popped into your mind! Your subconscious mind knew the name all along and merely needed to be primed.

## STOREHOUSE OF RICHES
## IN YOUR SUBCONSCIOUS MIND

This gold mine of your mind is stored within your subconscious mind. Every secret ever used by the world's richest men is stored there. Every technique used by investors in the stock market, real estate, or other commodities is known to your subconscious mind. It has inherited a kind of genetic and cosmic storehouse of memory and can help boost your own level of money-knowledge if you enlist its aid.

During the Depression years when money was scarce and jobs were nonexistent, a man had a terrific need for money. He was married and a baby was on the way, and he couldn't even find work. However, this man drew on the power of his subconscious mind to give him ideas for future wealth.

In the hours of waiting for his luck to change, he and his wife devised a little game built around money, in which they visualized they were millionaires. They set up a miniature area duplicating Atlantic City, where they had spent happy vacations in more prosperous times. They devised houses and hotels and street signs, and then played at being millionaires, buying and selling these various pieces of real estate. They called their little game Monopoly. When their friends played it with them, they suggested that they try to market the interesting game. Charles Darrow began to demonstrate his new game in stores in Philadelphia and people bought it by the hundreds. Soon a national distributor began to manufacture it on a large scale and it sold nationally and internationally. Charles Darrow and his family became rich through this idea that sprang from his subconscious mind when his need became pressing.

**Rule No. 1.** When you have a money need do not sit around worrying about how to improve your lot in life. Sit quietly and think about the ideas that are stored in your subconscious mind waiting to be released and which can make you rich beyond your wildest dreams.

Then give your subconscious mind programming that will release these Golden Nuggets to your conscious mind. To program your subconscious mind, every morning when you awaken and every night, when you prepare to go to sleep, repeat the following subconscious suggestions:

> I wish to make a fortune. I ask for ideas from my subconscious mind that will make me rich.
> I can be a big success. I have faith in my future destiny.
> I will discover the one idea that can make me a million dollars.
> I can become a creative genius with the aid of my subconscious mind.
> I have the power to rise to great heights in my work.
> I ask my subconscious mind for creative ideas that will bring me a steady flow of money.

When you sit in regular periods of meditation and invoke the higher power of your subconscious mind, it will come to your aid and release the ideas that can make you rich.

Positive programming of your subconscious mind will bring immediate results. Your subconscious is a neutral agent that will carry out any commands that you give it.

A man who used his subconscious mind to give him a creative idea for making a million dollars had often thought about becoming rich. He did not have that one idea however, that could make him a big success. One night fate took a hand in triggering a million-dollar idea from his subconscious mind. A lawyer in New York City, Ralph E. Schneider, was out to dinner with friends one evening, when he found he had left his wallet in his other suit.

After he got out of that embarrassing situation through the aid of his friends, he began to ponder on some method by which a person could go anywhere with just a simple credit card that would be honored by hotels, restaurants and airlines. Out of this subconscious speculation came the multimillion-dollar idea for the Diners Club. The idea spread like wildfire until Schneider had 100,000 members with credit cards that were honored in thousands of restaurants, hotels, airlines, auto-rental companies, and other places of business from one coast to the other.

Rule No. 2. To tap the power of your subconscious mind write down on filing cards one new idea a day that you believe can help you make a fortune. Do not worry about how silly the idea may sound to you; when you begin the process of projecting your ideas from your subconscious mind, you may get that one million-dollar idea that can make you rich.

When you have accumulated a half-dozen or so of these filing cards, sit quietly each day and shuffle them, looking at them, letting each one jell for a few moments, until one idea will trigger action. This may be an idea for inventing some new product, or for selling something you already have thought of. It may be a new service you can bring to the public, or it may be some investment that you should make. Your subconscious mind will soon sort out all the usable ideas that are lodged in its depths and bring you the one that can make you rich.

A 40-year-old man, whose life had not been too successful, gave a great deal of thought to how he might make a fortune. Time was passing rapidly and he knew that he had only a few short years in which to originate some big idea that could make him a million dollars. His brother called him one day and told him that he had found a new way to paint, which would save a lot of time and was easier than the old brush method. He had tied lamb's wool on a stick and used this as a brush. It covered a larger area and went on more easily than with a brush.

That idea triggered Vern T. Touchett's subconscious mind. All his concentrating on some big idea to make him rich fell into place immediately. He suggested to his brother that they market a paint roller made of lamb's wool. Although paint rollers had been made before, they were all made with materials other than lamb's wool. When Latex-based paints came on the market the Touchett brothers had to come up with another type of roller that would not matt and smear. They did this by weaving a new material Dynel into their rollers and they now gross more than $10,000,000 a year, with prospects of one day going to as high as $50,000,000.

**Rule No. 3.** Do not stop after one or two discouraging experiences, for your subconscious mind will keep releasing other, better ideas, if one or two do not work.

Many people receive a brilliant idea from the subconscious mind and try it, but it does not always go over. Then they become discouraged and discard the idea entirely.

Sometimes it may be necessary to try and discard several ideas, but always sit and ask your subconscious mind for other ideas until you have the exact idea that suits your talents and your needs. If you give up too soon, your subconscious mind will soon stop trying to give you new ideas and will fall back into patterns of habitual failure and discouragement.

A prospector in Nevada in the early days of gold-mining discovered a claim that brought him a few thousand dollars worth of gold. Then the vein ran out and he sold his equipment to a junk man and gave up in his search for more gold. The junk man dug two feet further and opened a pocket of gold that brought him $40,000! In five years time this man had taken $5,000,000 worth of gold out of that gold mine!

Sometimes if you keep on just a short time longer, you will get an idea that can bring you a million dollars.

**Rule No. 4.** Build success and money-attracting habits in your subconscious mind by dwelling daily on thoughts that deal with money. Absorb information from the stock market section of your daily paper. Acquaint yourself with the names of stocks on the big board. Read *The Wall Street Journal* and saturate your subconscious mind with success stories of people who have made millions through their business ability. Read *Fortune* magazine and let the articles stimulate your subconscious mind with the success theme, so it will release to your conscious mind an idea that can make you rich.

Create a subconscious Money Chest in which you practice the art of accumulating money and other treasures. Put into that Money Chest the equivalent of $1,000,000 in a form that will be easy to count every day until you build the subconscious habit of thinking in terms of big money. Cut out 10 pieces of white paper in the shape and size of a regular dollar bill. Write in the four corners of this paper $100,000 and copy the wording from a dollar bill: Federal Reserve Note; The United States of America; This note is legal tender for all debts, public and private. Then in the oval for the picture write the name of Woodrow Wilson. His face is actually on the original $100,000 bill which I have seen in New York City at the Chase Manhattan Money Museum.

When you have completed these 10 bills for $100,000 dollars, you have the total sum of $100,000,000. Each night, in order to build money awareness, count these 10 bills over and begin to get the feel of how much $100,000 is and how much a half-million and one million dollars actually are.

Then mentally take certain sums of money and invest them in the stock market, buying stocks on paper and watching their value go up. Trade these stocks for others, until you have built awareness of what it is to trade in large sums of money.

Buy certain pieces of real estate with your million dollars. Invest in your dream home, buy that car you want to drive; take that dream tour you want by getting travel literature and pasting it in your Scrapbook of Destiny, and getting all the information you can on such interesting places as Hawaii, Egypt, India, Europe, Australia . . . wherever you feel you want to go. Soon you will be guided by your subconscious mind to taking that trip, and the money will come in the most peculiar ways

## HOW A WOMAN WAS GUIDED
## TO A ROUND THE WORLD CRUISE

A woman I once knew was a manicurist in a beauty salon. She had an intense desire to go around the world but never saved enough to even go to Europe on her vacation. I told her this subconscious secret for attracting money or its equivalent. She went to a travel agency and got literature about a cruise going around the world at a price she could never afford.

She began to concentrate on these pictures of her dream tour every day for 15 minutes. One day she was impelled to go back to the travel agency. She talked to the woman, and told her she wanted to take the round the world cruise but she had no money. She told her she was a manicurist and asked if there was any chance she might get a job on the ship.

The woman sent her to a big steamship line where she made application to work in the beauty salon, and she was hired. This woman, without a penny in the bank, embarked on a new adventure on her round the world trip. But the greatest surprise still lay ahead of her. A man became seasick on the ship and she read to him every day. He fell in love with her and married her before they landed in New York! He took her to a jewelry store on Fifth Avenue and asked her to pick out something she liked from a tray of diamonds. She chose a very modest little diamond engagement ring. He said, "Is there anything else you would like?"

Jokingly, she replied, "Yes, I'd like the whole tray of diamonds!"

The man replied, "Fine, we'll take them all!"

To this woman's surprise she later found out that the man she had fallen in love with was a multimillionaire, and he actually bought her a million dollars worth of diamonds as a wedding gift! This woman is now one of the leading society women in Bel-Air society in California, and has helped raise millions of dollars for charity.

**Rule No. 5.** Create a strong magnet within your subconscious mind to attract large sums of money to you. You can do this by making out a check for a million dollars, payable to yourself, and signed, God, the Universal Banker. Then when you do your money treatment each day, look at that million dollar check and give yourself this subconscious programming:

> I now claim my divine inheritance from the universal bank of riches and abundance. I desire the sum of $5,000 within the next year from an unexpected source. I wish to have money to put down on a house, to buy a car, to own a color TV set, and furnishings for my home. I have faith that this money will come to me in the near future.

You should carry this million dollar check with you at all times. Look at it several times a day, and claim from this universal storehouse of riches the various sums of money you need from time to time. Give yourself this money ritual when you have any special needs and then keep a small notebook in which you list the various sums of money you do receive. These may be small at first, but gradually, when you total the various sums over a year, you will probably discover they are bigger than you think.

A lecture member did this in New York City. She put down that she wanted the sum of $1,000 within two months. She was given a raise in salary within two weeks which totaled $250 in a year. Someone gave her a TV set that she needed, and this being a color TV set, she put down the equivalent value of

$300. The TV set had actually cost over $1,000 when it was new.

At Christmas, which was within a month from the time she had started her bookkeeping, she received cash and gifts totaling $750. Already, in less than two months she had attracted more than the original $1,000 she had put down on her list. She began a new list, this time putting down $2,000. A few days later a check for $500 came to her from a wealthy uncle who lived in California. The money began to pour in, and when it was not money, she found that money equivalents came to her from the most unexpected sources, until finally she had her sum of $2,000.

**Rule No. 6.** To dredge up the golden nuggets that are stored in your subconscious mind, program your subconscious each day with positive money motivators.

Repeat at least 10 times every morning and night the following money motivators:

I will make a fortune.
I can become a great success.
I will get an idea that will make me a million dollars.
I have creative power within my mind.
I do and say the things that will attract money to me.
I create great things through the power of my mind.
I attract money from many different sources.

A housewife told me once at a lecture that she had no special talent and was so busy taking care of her two children that she simply could not go out and work. She and her husband needed more money as inflation had cut into their savings. She asked me how she could possibly attract more money under these limiting circumstances.

I quoted from the Bible, "What hast thou in thine house?" Then I asked her what she could do best. She laughingly said, "I make beautiful pies, cakes and pastries, but who wants to get fat eating them?"

I told this woman to sit down each day and ask her subconscious mind for an idea to make extra money which fit her unique talent, which, in this case, was baking pastries.

One day she got an idea to put an ad in the neighborhood paper saying she would bake cakes for birthday parties and special occasions, She had some cards printed, and began to distribute them in apartment house mailboxes near her home. Within a few days time orders began to come in and from this simple beginning she built a business that was bringing in all the extra money her family needed!

**Rule No. 7.** To aid your subconscious mind in releasing the golden nuggets that are stored within, write down on filing cards a new idea each day for making money. Do not feel any idea is foolish, but when it comes to you, write it down. Then store these filing cards in a small box, and when you have ten or twenty of them, shuffle them over and look through them one at a time, until one or more will trigger subconscious action within your mind.

**Rule No. 8.** Use the money pump exercise to stir your subconscious mind with creative action to release ideas that can make you rich.

When I was a boy on the farm, we used to have a pump in the yard that had to be primed by pouring some water into it, and then the flow of water began.

Your subconscious mind sometimes needs a primer to release its creative energy to show you how to make a fortune.

Start the flow of creative energy from your subconscious mind by doing this:

A. Imagine something you want to do, for which you need money, and then let your mind dwell on the methods you would use to fill this money need. As you begin to think along these lines your subconscious mind will be primed to release its stored up ideas for your enrichment.

B. Mentally think of something you can do to fill a basic human need, and ideas will begin to flow from your subconscious mind. Someone primed his mind with the idea that brought about the can opener. Another person invented plastics by seeing the need for bottles that would not break. Still another found a basic need that caused him to invent the telephone. The flow of golden ideas from the subconscious mind is always stimulated by searching for something that people need.

C. Prime your subconscious mind with inspiration from the lives of great men and women. Read the stories of their successes and then strive to emulate the great thoughts they have released to the world. The lives of Edison, Lincoln, Leonardo da Vinci, Michelangelo, Galileo, Columbus, Newton, and other geniuses will help the subconscious flow of ideas to be released from your own subconscious mind bringing your own potentials into sharper focus.

D. Look around you, in your own environment, in your own work, there may be hidden treasures which you have not been aware of. Count your blessings and as you do, you will create the causative links in the chain of success that will release Golden Nuggets of precious ideas from your subconscious mind to bring you greater wealth.

## POINTS TO REMEMBER

1. The valuable Hidden Vein of Gold exists in your subconscious mind, and can make you rich.
2. A man's financial needs created the game Monoply which brought him fame and riches in a few years time.
3. Program your subconscious mind with ideas that can start the flow of gold in your own life.
4. The subconscious mind can create riches out of seeming defeat, through financial emergencies. The famous Diners Club idea came through such a source.

5. Start the flow of riches from the hidden depths of your subconscious mind by writing down on filing cards each idea that comes to you for making money.

6. A 40-year-old man now makes $10,000,000 a year because he tapped the power of his subconscious mind and came up with the idea for painting with a roller made of Dynel.

7. Go that extra few feet when exploring for the gold of your subconscious mind. A gold prospector in Nevada lost a fortune of $5,000,000 because he did not dig two feet more!

8. Build success and money habits by reading the big money journals and discovering how others have made millions.

9. Build a subconscious Money Chest in which you put the equivalent of $1,000,000 and count out what you need each night, until you have built the subconscious money habit.

10. A woman was guided to a round the world tour and met a wealthy man she later married through her subconscious desire to have money.

11. Build a strong money magnet within your subconscious mind that can attract large sums of money to you.

12. A woman attracted the sum of $1,000 within two months through using the law of mental equivalents where she visualized a color TV set and other objects which actually came to her.

13. Use the seven subconscious money motivators to dredge up the Golden Nuggets that are stored in your subconscious mind.

14. Use the money pump exercise to stir your subconscious mind to release the golden ideas that can make you rich.

15. The four dynamic money primers can release a flood of money from your subconscious mind.

# 10 WAYS YOU CAN
# MAGNETIZE MONEY AND
# BECOME A MONEY MAGNET

# 7

In my study of 10,000 men and women who have magnetized money and become enormously rich, I discovered that they actually used certain techniques to magnetize money. You can use these same techniques and magnetize money, or money equivalents in houses, land, jewels, cars, furs, or other material treasures.

I once visited the U.S. mint in the days when they were still turning out gold pieces. The tour director showed us a series of machines which were busily turning out pennies, nickles, dimes, quarters, half-dollars and dollars. In the penny machine a steady strip of copper was converted into pennies by a die that was especially made to press out pennies. In the dollar machine, a steady strip of silver was converted into bright, shiny silver dollars. One machine, however, was being fed a strip of glistening, yellow gold and it was turning out brand-new $20 gold pieces. This was the machine that interested me most.

What was the difference, I asked myself, between the

penny machine and the $20 machine? The machines were the same, but the imprint on the die of each machine was different. Also, the type of metal being fed into the two machines was entirely different. One was copper, the other was solid gold.

## YOUR MIND IS A MONEY-MAKING MACHINE!

From that simple discovery I evolved my theory that the human mind is actually a money-making machine. You involve into your mind certain concepts and these evolve as your destiny. Some people magnetize their minds with copper-plated ideas; they turn out mediocre talents and they attract small salaries and cheap destinies. Other people have learned how to involve the golden ideas in consciousness that magnetize their minds with value and importance.

Your brain, the machine that helps you magnetize money, is the same as the brain of an Onassis or Rockefeller. The only thing that is different is the value that you are stamping on that brain, the golden ideas or the copper-plated, penny ideas that bring a shoddy destiny and poverty. If you know how to program your higher mind centers with the pure gold of creative thoughts, you will produce from your life experiences money, fame, success, friends, love, happiness—all the treasures of life that man requires to have a happy destiny.

There are 10 ways you can magnetize your mind to turn out the shining, golden ideas that can bring you a fortune. This is done by programming your higher mind centers with certain verbs of action that communicate golden ideas to your sympathetic nervous system. These ideas are then evolved in your daily words and actions, leading you to achieve that which you have first conceived.

## HOW A WOMAN MAGNETIZED HER MIND WITH FAILURE

A woman who came into my lecture in Los Angeles complained that she was poverty-stricken. She said, "Everything

I touch turns to brass. Other people buy property and it goes up in value. I bought land and sold it. Now its worth millions. I married and thought it was true love; it ended in divorce. I invested money in the market; it went down and I lost it all. I seem to be on the losing end all the time!"

It took me only a few moments to analyze why this woman was on the losing side of life instead of the winning side.

She was negatively programmed to defeat, disaster and despair. Her every word showed she involved only thoughts of loss, lack and limitation. I gave her the 10 magnetizing statements for money, which she began to use at once. The first week she reported to me that she received $1,000 from a source she had thought was lost. A man who borrowed money to go into business had a big success and gave her back the $500 he had borrowed, with a $500 bonus! She had changed the polarity of her higher mind from negative to positive and money began to flow from unexpected sources!

### THE TEN MAGNETIC PROGRAMMERS
### THAT CAN MAKE YOU RICH

**1. I desire money or its equivalents.**

When you desire food something drives you in the direction where that food may be obtained. This follows the well-known law of self-preservation.

When you desire love fulfillment, you magnetize the mind centers with love and attract your soul mate.

The same law of magnetism applies to money and its attraction. The key words "I Desire" help program your higher mind centers with whatever you wish to attract.

Sit quietly and involve this magnetic programming statement in your consciousness. Repeat the following statement at least 10 times, saying the words to yourself slowly.

I desire money or its equivalents to achieve the following

objectives in my life. I wish to have an income of $50,000 a
year so I may do the things I want, take trips, have leisure time
for cultural pursuits, help my family, educate my children,
buy a home of my own in which to entertain my friends. I
desire money so I may buy a new car that I need for my work
and pleasure. I desire the sum of $2,000 within the next three
months so I may clear up my bills and pay on my mortgage. I
desire beautiful clothes, fine jewelry, a color TV set, and
furnishings for my home. I have faith the money will come to
me to have all these things.

When you do your mental programming with the key
words "I Desire," you can read any of these programming
statements to yourself, or make up your own to signify the
things you want money for.

You can make this mental programming more forceful by
writing down the specific desires you have for money and then
reading them over each morning and each night. As you go to
sleep at night, keep repeating the desires to yourself until they
are firmly lodged in your subconscious mind.

## HOW A WOMAN MAGNETIZED EXTRA INCOME

Betty J. was a young woman of 25 and had been married
and divorced before she was 23. She had a big ambition to
become a writer but she had no spare time to write. She began
to program her higher mind with the "I Desire" statements.

She added to the list of programming statements, "I desire
an income as a writer of fiction and articles." She put this down
on a sheet of paper and began to read it every morning and
night, saying it often during her day, while she worked as a
secretary in a manufacturing concern.

Within two weeks time Betty was talking to a friend who
told her that a big apartment house where she lived needed a
manager. Something clicked in Betty's mind. If she were an
apartment house manager she knew she would get an apartment
and a small salary, giving her enough leisure time for writing.

She applied for the job and got it. The apartment was large and comfortable and her duties simple—she showed vacant apartments. A janitor did all the work and a gardener took care of the spacious gardens. She had a beautiful environment in which to dream up her ideas for articles and stories. The first month she was on her new job she wrote an article on how young divorcees could successfully manage their lives and it sold for $400. From this beginning she went on to write the novel which she had been laboring over for three years. It was finished in six months; her agent sold her first novel to a publisher; and the galley proofs were sold to a motion picture company for $85,000! Betty J. is now on the way to becoming one of our most important young writers!

### 2. I become successful and important.

If you are struggling to win recognition and feel constantly discouraged and defeated, use this subconscious programmer. It will help program your higher mind centers with thoughts of your value and importance. It will change your self-image from failure to success. It will help raise your self-esteem and give you the confidence you may need to meet life's challenges with courage and faith.

The verb *to be* is one of dynamic action. The moment you state "I am," you start a flow of creative action in your higher mind centers. When you state, "I am important; I am successful; I become rich through my creative efforts," you are expressing dynamic mind power along the lines of success.

Contrarily, when you state "I am a failure; I am only worth $150 a week; I am not worthy of the better things of life," you short-circuit the magnetism of your brain cells and become that which you believe and express.

Use this mental programmer to give yourself the mental boost you require to raise yourself from ordinary levels of creative action to extraordinary ones. The only difference between geniuses and ordinary people is that geniuses do not ask how to become great.

A young boy of 10 approached the great composer Mozart after a concert and said, "Maestro, how can I become a great composer like you?"

The genius replied, "I'm sorry, but I do not know how to tell you to become a great composer."

The boy persisted, "But Maestro, when you were 10 you were composing symphonies."

Mozart replied, "Yes, my boy, I was, but I did not have to ask anyone how to."

So too in your own life, you can program yourself with the statement "I become successful and important," and you will be guided by your higher mind to the unfolding of the exact talent you have to make you great.

Repeat the following programming statements of dynamic action to elevate yourself to the right level of creative effort.

> I become successful and important. I raise my level of creative action from mediocre to superior quality. I change my self-image from one of failure to one of success. I become original in my thinking and project new ideas that can make me a million dollars.

### 3. I attract money or its equivalents.

This powerful programming statement actually stirs the psycho-neuro centers of your brain with dynamic, creative action. You make your mind a magnet by involving in it the thoughts that magnetize money. You project the following statements with the "I Attract" programmer:

> I attract money or its equivalents. I know that money is important to have, for with it I can do much good. I attract work that will give me a chance to make a bigger salary.
> I shall be guided to a business of my own, or a creative idea that can make me rich. One invention has made a million for some people. One song or novel can make a million dollars. One creative impulse can guide me to my fortune

I project something of value to the world and I expect to receive adequate rewards in terms of money or money equivalents.

I attract important people and they recognize my worth and help me achieve my money goals. I attract opportunities through people of wealth and position and I become elevated to my proper place in life.


## HOW A YOUNG GIRL ATTRACTED MONEY

A young girl of 20 came to New York City from Greece. She had learned to speak English and attended some of my lectures and classes. She began to program herself to attract some rich person who could help her find her right place where she could make a good salary and improve her situation socially.

She met a young doctor who told her he knew of an elderly woman who was a semi-invalid, who needed someone to be a companion and secretary. The elderly woman was a wealthy Greek, the mother of a very famous ship owner. The girl applied and got the job. She stayed with this woman five years and was able to live in the most luxurious environments, travel, and accumulate money. The old woman often gave her extra bonuses at Christmas and other special occasions. The girl finally had several thousand dollars in the bank and she kept programming her higher mind with the thought she would meet a suitable mate and marry. One day the nephew of the elderly woman came for a visit from Greece. He met the young girl and fell in love with her. They had a big wedding and the girl became a member of the wealthy ship owners family! Your good will seek you out if you program your higher mind centers with the "I Attract" programmer.

**4. I win success and riches in the game of life.**

This positive mental programmer can be used to change the polarity of your magnetism from losing to winning, from failure to success, from poverty to riches. Magnetism has two polarities—one negative, the other positive.

Some people are on the negative polarity of magnetism; they push their luck away from them. They lose friends, they discourage love, they polarize failure instead of success.

A young man came to me for counselling. His life story was a dismal one of failure, defeat and unhappiness. He showed me a tattoo which he had had engraved on his right arm which said, "BORN TO LOSE." He said this was truly prophetic of his life. He was always on the losing end, never the winning side of life.

This young man had actually inscribed on his mind the words "BORN TO LOSE." The constant repetition of that unmagnetic statement, every time he saw it on his arm, actually impressed his subconscious mind with the negative thought of failure.

I knew another man who had something tattooed on his chin when he was a young man and became intoxicated. He had one star on each side of his chin, and he told his sailor companions that he was going to one day become a two-star admiral. The other sailors laughed and after the tattooing job was finished they went back to their ship and forgot the entire incident. But the young sailor who had the two stars tattooed on his chin never forgot this drunken prank, and to cover up his mistake he grew a small goatee. Years later this man actually became a two-star admiral in the United States Navy!

To utilize the "I Win" magnetic statement, repeat the following statement and imprint it on your subconscious mind. When it is once programmed there for good, you simply state the words "I Win" whenever you want to invoke its magnetism for attracting money or winning out in any situation in life.

I win out in the game of life. I imprint my higher mind with success thoughts. I win friends, I win love, I win money and its equivalents. I am playing for high stakes in the game of life

and I want to be on the winning side. I win out in my right
work for a good salary, promotions and benefits. I invest
money and win security for my future. I hold the winning
concept in my mind and I attract positive experiences, helpful
friends and constructive ideas that will make me rich.

### 5. I believe in myself and my future great destiny.

The "I Believe" programming helps you overcome doubt
and fear. It removes self-consciousness and feelings of inferiority that might have been programmed in your consciousness
when you were young.

To erase this type of negative programming, use the above
positive programming statement as follows:

I believe in myself and my future great destiny. What others
have done I also can achieve. I now program my subconscious
mind to thoughts of riches and success. I can and will overcome
all limitations in my life. I rise above my limitations of
education and environment. I release the power of my subconscious and superconscious minds and possess adequate knowledge to achieve my great destiny.

I once met a young veteran who returned from war with
both arms shot off. He was very bitter and viewed his future
prospects with hopelessness. I gave him the mental programming that he could still find himself and achieve success.

He told me he had planned on becoming a writer, but how
could he write without arms? I gave him some programming
statements to use, telling him that his higher mind would find a
way to release his creative talents if he really believed in
himself. When I returned to visit him two weeks later this
armless man had bought an electric typewriter and was labori-
ously learning how to type with his toes! The astounding thing
is that he finally achieved this miracle and wrote a book, which
was accepted and published! Motion pictures bought the book

and now this veteran is on the way to achieving his dream of becoming a writer.

The newspapers carried an account of another veteran who was without arms. He learned how to paint by holding a brush in his teeth! Some of his paintings have been exhibited in a big gallery and he has sold everything he has painted to date.

### 6. I command and control my mind, my environment, other people and my destiny.

This positive mental programming statement should be used whenever you want to gain complete control of yourself and your destiny. Order and harmony exist when you are able to assume control of your mind, your body, your habits, and your environment.

Use the following positive programming statements to put your mind under control. Then project this same power to your environment. When you meet other people you can use this power to cause them to do your bidding by making your silent statements of command and control.

> I now command and control my mind and my body. I possess a center of power within myself that yields to my desires and aspirations. I wish to magnetize money and success. I realize that all my success will come to me through other people. I now project the power of my personality to everyone I meet, reflecting charm, courtesy, goodness, peace, poise and quality.

### 7. I enrich my mind with money concepts and my life becomes prosperous and successful.

This programmer can be used whenever you want to increase the flow of money or its equivalents in your life. Because this dynamic verb of action encompasses the word rich, it will soon penetrate deep in your consciousness releasing other related ideas about money and success that will drive you in the direction of a fortune.

Use the following "I Enrich" programmer to start the flow of creative mental energy in the direction of money power and success.

> I enrich my mind with money concepts and my life becomes prosperous and successful. I enrich my mind with knowledge from many sources. I magnetize the centers of my consciousness with money power and I attract money and its equivalents. I enrich the world with my flow of constructive and creative ideas and the world compensates me according to my true worth. I am in the flow of money, success, happiness, love fulfillment and all the true riches that make life worthwhile.

### 8. I overcome obstacles, problems and obstructions in my pathway to success.

This powerful mental conditioner will program your higher mind centers with the drive and determination to overcome the difficulties that often arise on the pathway to riches and success.

When you realize that most great people have had to overcome tremendous handicaps on their rise to fame and riches, you can be encouraged to know that you too can overcome whatever obstacles fate places in your path.

The late President Roosevelt had polio and yet he was able to become one of the world's most influential men, winning presidential office four times, when other people might have given up the moment that crippling disease struck them.

Edison was deaf and instead of accepting this as a curse that blighted his entire life, he turned it into a blessing. He claimed he could concentrate better on his work because of this affliction.

Shakespeare was the uneducated son of a butcher, yet he was able to overcome these limitations and become one of the world's greatest playwrights.

George Washington Carver was born to slave parents, and

yet he overcame the circumstances of his early environment to become one of the nation's greatest agricultural experts and scientists.

Always we find in a study of the lives of the great that there was a tremendous obstacle that had to be overcome in their triumphant rise to fame, fortune and achievement.

Use the following mental programmer when you want to overcome some situation in your life that is hindering you on your pathway to power and riches.

I overcome obstacles, problems and obstructions in my pathway to success. I grow stronger with every challenge. I build character from the challenges of life and grow stronger mentally and spiritually. I overcome my negative habits and am able to concentrate more thoroughly on success and money power. I overcome the influences of discouraging people who try to hold me back and rise to my true stature of greatness and achievement.

## POINTS TO REMEMBER

1. Your mind is a money-making machine, stamping out in dollars and cents your true worth. Learn how to make it stamp out a fortune through magnetism.
2. A woman magnetized her mind with fear and failure and attracted these things until I showed her how to re-cycle her mind with positive ideas of riches.
3. The magnetic programmers can make you rich, by using the emotion of desire for money and its equivalents.
4. A young woman used this magnetic programmer and sold her first novel to a motion picture company for $85,000.
5. A young Greek girl came to New York and used this money magnetizer to attract a wealthy employer and through this woman she met and married the son of a shipping tycoon.

6. Change your polarity of mind from a poor, negative one, to a rich, positive one that brings you a fortune.

7. An armless veteran used this secret to become a writer, using his feet to operate an electric typewriter.

8. Use the art of command and control to program yourself into mental habits of success.

9. Use this power of magnetism to overcome obstacles and solve problems and obstructions that stand in your way to riches.

10. Great men have overcome their afflictions by using this magnetic programmer and have achieved fame and immortality.

# LAW OF THE DOUBLE RETURN---
## DOUBLE YOUR MONEY,
## DOUBLE YOUR LUCK
## FOR FINANCIAL INDEPENDENCE

# 8

You can utilize a powerful cosmic law to double your money and double your luck. This cosmic law works everywhere in nature. When you plant a kernel of corn it does not produce one kernel but will yield a whole stalk of corn. A single grain of wheat produces a stalk that might have as many as fifty or more kernels. When you plant a pint of wheat it produces a bushel. Always the law of the harvest decrees that you shall reap more than you have sown.

You can use this same cosmic law to magnetize money or its equivalents in goods and possessions.

When you put a seed thought of money in your mind, it will branch out and associate with the other thoughts imprinted on your subconscious mind. When these thoughts gather momentum they are suddenly projected from your subconscious mind through your conscious mind and cause you to do the things that will make money for you.

When I was living on a farm as a young man, I used to plant potatoes in the spring. We would cut a potato up in sections that each had a seed or eye in it. That single seed would produce in the fall a whole cluster of perfect potatoes. The law of multiple return was at work in the seed and in the soil.

God blesses His universe with this law of abundance on all planes. It works for you, when you know how to invoke it, to bring you money, houses, land, jewels, cars, and things of value. Money obeys this law of the double return and will multiply and grow under the impetus of magnetism.

## REGIMEN TO DOUBLE YOUR MONEY
## AND DOUBLE YOUR LUCK

1. Sit down each day and spend five minutes in concentrating on money or its equivalents in goods and possessions. Make up your mind that for that one day you are going to plant seed money and ask for double the amount you give out.

Start first with a dollar bill. Take the dollar and fold it in the shape of a pyramid, over the picture on the back of the dollar bill of the pyramid and the eye in its center. This pyramid is an occult symbol placed on the dollar bill by President Franklin Roosevelt. It is based on esoteric knowledge that is in the pyramid of Gizeh in Egypt. The four sides of the pyramid are represented by the words faith, hope, charity and love. The eye at the peak of the pyramid is the all-seeing eye of God, and also represents the third eye or psychic center in man's consciousness that can guide you to success and enrichment.

When you have folded your dollar in the shape of a pyramid, be sure that the pyramid printed on the dollar bill is right in the center of your pyramid that you have folded. Then bless this dollar bill as you sit in meditation, using these mystical words:

I now bless this symbol of God's creative power and release it
to do good in the world. I invoke the mystical qualities of
faith, hope, charity and love, as I bless this money and release
it to work the law of the double return for me. I ask that this
dollar multiply and grow under the law of the harvest bringing
me a ten-fold yield. I release it joyously, invoking the cosmic
law of the double return.

2. When you have blessed the dollar bill and folded it in
the shape of the mystical pyramid, give it to some charity, or a
blind person. You may give it to your church, the Cancer Fund,
Lighthouse for the Blind, a veterans' organization, or any other
worthy charity. When you give it make the declaration that the
money will come back to you in a period of 10 days under the
law of tithing or the law of the harvest. This law is given in the
Bible and works miracles for people who use it.

3. Utilize nature's three elements through the golden law
of alchemy to increase your money.

**A. The seed or egg principle.** This process of forming the
mental seed for doubling your money is known as ingestion. Put
into your mind the thought that you want money and its
equivalents. Sit and concentrate on what you want to do with
the money. Do not mentally visualize money in itself, but see
yourself buying the dream home you desire. Visualize yourself
furnishing it. See in your mind's eye the color television set you
want. Mentally project the dream of the car you would like to
own. See yourself driving it, taking your family and friends for
a drive to some special place.

The law of alchemy that works in nature to enrich the
earth takes the sunshine and converts its golden substance into
food in the soil and on trees and vines. It takes a tiny acorn and
makes it a giant oak tree. The tree weighs 2 billion times more
than the acorn from which it came. Where did the substance
come from that could produce such a giant tree? The law of

cosmic alchemy working in sun, rain and soil produces the miracles of life.

The same law of cosmic alchemy takes an orange seed and produces a golden orange that nourishes us. From the same patch of black soil comes a green and pink watermelon with black seed, as well as a patch of white cotton, red raspberries, crimson tomatoes, green lettuce and pink roses. What power in the soil creates these living miracles? It is the infinite intelligence of a divine mind that works through its creation to produce what man requires to give him life and fulfillment of his destiny.

This same law of cosmic alchemy will work to bring you money or its equivalents. Ingestion of the thought or creative idea in your mind will start the process of alchemy working. The Bible gives this law: "As ye sow, so shall ye reap." The thought or seed you put in consciousness will produce the equivalent of the seed or thought in your own life.

## HOW A MAN MADE A MILLION
## THROUGH MENTAL ALCHEMY

A young artist got tired of cleaning his palette of old, hard paint. It took so long to clean it that it limited his work. He sat in silent meditation for a few days, asking his higher mind to give him an idea that would save him from the monotonous chore of cleaning his palette each day. One day an idea came through his subconscious mind to get a piece of oil paper and put it on his palette. He squeezed his colors on the paper and when he finished his days work, he simply threw away the paper. From this idea came the paper palette that is widely used by artists. This simple idea made the originator a millionaire!

B. Use the cosmic law of absorption to double your money and double your luck. When the seed has been planted in the ground, it takes a little while for the soil to absorb it. The magnetic impulses of the soil flow through the seed releasing chemistry within it that causes it to break out of its prison shell and absorb the right elements from the soil to make it a perfect tree or flower or vegetable.

Likewise, when you have planted the seeds of money and its equivalents in your mind, you must give them time to sprout, grow roots and begin to mature. If you become impatient and abandon your mental crop it will die without producing its harvest.

Put into your mind knowledge and wisdom. You must magnetize your mind centers with creative ideas that will start the flow of mental energy that can produce riches for you.

Go to the library and get books on the lives of great people who have achieved fortunes and study their lives. Learn from them the secret power they used. If you want to make a fortune by being an artist, study the lives of great artists and get their inspiration for your own creative efforts.

If you would like to become an author, study the lives of great writers from Shakespeare right down to the modern authors like Harold Robbins, Norman Mailer and Jacqueline Susann, to mention a few.

If you want to make a fortune through inventions, absorb ideas from the lives of great inventors like Edison. If you want to make a million dollars by composing popular or classical music, study the lives and works of Mozart, Chopin, Beethoven, or some of our modern composers like Irving Berlin, George Gershwin, Cole Porter and Bachrach. You will absorb inspiration and creative ideas by stimulating your mind centers with the creative ideas that made these men great.

If you want to become a millionaire by being an industrialist or manufacturer, get books on the lives of men who have made millions, like Rockefeller, Howard Hughes, J. Paul Getty, Onassis and J.P. Morgan.

Absorb money ideas by studying the financial pages of

your newspaper. Read magazines like *Fortune* and *Forbes* which carry success stories of successful people.

A young man who came to some of our classes in New York wanted to make a million dollars. He had been raised on a farm where his father raised cattle. He loved animals and made up his mind he would work with horses. He began to absorb all the knowledge he could about breeding fine horses. He studied animal husbandry and learned the latest techniques about breeding race horses. He saved his money and in two years time he had enough to buy a race horse at an eastern track through a claiming race. The horse was from good stock, so he began to breed the mare with a well-known race horse that was now in service. The second colt born to this mare matured into a fine race horse and began to win her first races. In time this horse won half a million dollars in stakes and the young man is now on his way to making his first million dollars!

C. **Use the cosmic law of projection to release your creative ideas that can make you rich.** When you have ingested and absorbed creative ideas that can make you rich and successful, you must then complete the magnetic trinity by projecting these ideas through dynamic action. You cannot sit quietly and wait for money to come to you. You must project your golden ideas each day in a pattern of dynamic action.

Start the first day by sitting in meditation for five or ten minutes and deciding how you can begin immediately to release your creative ideas in your personal life. Is there some way you can improve your present work? Think of five ideas for selling your product to the public. Write down a list of prospective customers and write them letters invoking their assistance in your work. Dream up new techniques that you might use that can increase your income.

## A MAN MADE A MILLION DOLLARS
## THROUGH THIS METHOD

A young man studied cosmetology and entered the field as a hair stylist. He soon found that the world was filled with excellent beauticians who had more experience than he had. He worked for one year and found he was getting nowhere rapidly. He came to some of our classes and learned about the secrets for magnetizing money and projecting his golden ideas in his work.

He sat in meditation a few moments a day asking his higher mind to give him some idea that would make him a big success in the beauty field. One day the idea came to him to call himself a beauty diagnostician and give a careful analysis to each customer as to their exact needs in face care, hair styling and make-up. The first day that the sign was put in the beauty parlor window he had 20 customers at $25 each! From this beginning he was soon made a partner of the beauty salon and within two years he had begun his own string of beauty salons and had a staff of 50 people working for him. Not only did he train people in styling and specialized beauty services but he had a whole fleet of operators using his methods of diagnosis. After the diagnosis each woman ordered her beauty products and had her work done at one of his salons. In the short time of five years this young man sold out his entire chain of beauty salons for over a million dollars!

4. Accustom your mind to think in terms of big money and big ideas.

Most people are accustomed to think in limited terms of five, 10 or 20 dollars. They carefully count out their money each week after being paid and think of how they can stretch their dollars to go further. They build the subconscious money habit of limitation.

Expand your thinking to bigger money through this magnetic regimen: Cut out pieces of paper and label them in the four corners $20, $50 and $100. Now begin the process of multiplying these bills by doubling them. First you will have $40 when you double your $20 bill. Then you will have $80 when you double this $40. Now you will graduate to $160 and you will have to use your $100 and $50 bills and also cut out some that you label $10. When you double your $160 you will have the sum of $320. Now when you double this $320 three

more times you will have the sums of $640, $1280, and $2,560.
To play the game further and help magnetize your brain centers
with money power you will now need to cut out bills that you
label $1,000 and $5,000 and even $10,000. Keep on doubling
this simulated money until you have reached the figure of
$1,000,000 or more.

5. Now take your paper money and begin to write down in
a ledger the property you want to purchase. Look up a list of
properties in the local paper and begin to purchase a home, a
business, a farm, a car, or anything else that you would like to
own. Write down the sums of money you will pay for these
various properties. Soon your mind will begin to expand in the
direction of owning valuable property.

6. When you have used the doubling technique to magnetize your mind centers with big money concepts, enter into
your ledger the amount of stocks you want to buy, keeping a
careful record of your purchases. Also enter the sums you will
expend for diamonds, pearls, rubies, emeralds or any other
jewelry you desire. Write down the amount you will expend on
your furnishings for your dream home. Also record any trips
that you want to take, keeping a record of the costs and even
entering the travel literature in your ledger of the places you
want to visit.

7. When you have recorded all your money transactions
and a list of the things you want to buy, make out an inventory
of your possessions, cash reserves in the bank, and monthly
payments on apartment houses or other properties you purchase. Look these over every day, add up your total of
purchases, and have the expanded feeling that these things are
already in the universe and that you are magnetizing them and
will attract them in the future.

8. Now begin the process of applying the doubling technique to your everyday life. Start the morning by putting a $5
bill in a special place. Call this the golden egg for that day, and

ask your higher mind to double that amount through an unexpected source for that day. This may come about in the strangest ways; it does not always come as money, but may come as a gift, or theater tickets, or some piece of furniture that someone gives you. Count this as money for it has an equivalent value.

A woman began this process of doubling her money each day. She started out with a $5 bill, which she placed in a box, labeling it her golden nest egg. Within one week's time she had received the following money and goods. A neighbor friend was moving and did not want to take their heavy color TV set. She offered the $500 set to this woman for $100. A letter came two days after she began her doubling process, with a check for $20 from an uncle in Indianapolis, telling her to buy some gifts for her two children. A friend had an old, stuffed chair that needed upholstering. She gave it to this woman for nothing. When it was upholstered, it was easily worth $250. She was taken to the theater by a friend who wanted someone to walk home with her at night. Her doubling process was working in the strangest ways, and when the momentum started it did not stop, but kept snowballing until this woman had more than $2,000 in cash or money equivalents!

9. Now that you have stretched your thinking in the direction of big money and equivalent values, expand the horizons of your mind further by taking flights of imagination into realms of unlimited riches.

Visualize how the Rockefellers live on their estates, and how they expend money to keep up their fleets of cars, yachts, and country and town homes.

Project your mind to how it must be to have the money power of a Conrad Hilton with his vast chain of hotels all over the world.

Visualize Buckingham Palace and how Queen Elizabeth

with all her money and power must feel walking through the 500 rooms of that vast palace.

Think of the White House in Washington, D.C. and how it must feel to be the first family of the land.

Then expand your mind to conceive of the vast amounts of money expended on the world's biggest bridges, the world's tallest buildings, the building of the Pyramids, the Parthenon, the Taj Mahal, and the Great Wall of China that is 1,600 miles long and took 400 years to build.

Visualize the great art galleries of the world filled with their Rembrandts, Titians, Michelangelos, da Vincis, and Gainsboroughs. Think of the billions of volumes of books in the world's greatest libraries, containing the world's great thoughts.

Mentally claim all the free public parks in your own city. Take possession of the transportation systems that can take you wherever you want to go. Visualize the great airlines with their giant planes taking you around the world, visiting some of the world's most magnificent historic sites.

As you double your mental concepts and increase your mind's power to concentrate and visualize these great treasures, you will be expanding the horizons of your mind and it will be much easier for you to visualize yourself having the simple things that you want to magnetize and attract.

## POINTS TO REMEMBER

1. The cosmic law works in nature to double and increase everything from a grain of wheat to an oak forest from the simple seed that is planted in the soil.

2. Spend five minutes a day on concentrating on money and its equivalents, utilizing the law of the double return to increase your own supply of wealth.

3. Magnetize a dollar bill by shaping it like a pyramid and invoking a special money blessing to increase it and bring you 10 dollars for every dollar spent.

4. A young artist magnetized a million dollars by using this law of the double return.

5. The cosmic law of absorption will release magnetic impulses that can bring you creative ideas that make you rich.

6. A young man used these magnetic principles to attract a million dollars by breeding race horses and selling them to rich people all over the country.

7. You can use the law of cosmic projection to release your golden ideas that can make you rich.

8. A young man used the law of double return to make a fortune through cosmetology by calling himself a beauty diagnostician and perfecting a technique to sell women beauty products that made him soon own a fleet of beauty salons, which he later sold for more than a million dollars.

9. Expand your money consciousness by learning how to double your money, utilizing pieces of paper on which you write various sums from $10 to $1,000 until your mind is able to think in terms of thousands and millions.

10. Apply the doubling techniques to your everyday life by using the golden nest egg principle, and starting to magnetize your money and doubling it each day.

11. A woman used this technique to receive $2,000 in cash and money equivalents within a period of a few weeks.

12. Learn how to stretch your thinking in the direction of big money and its equivalents by visualizing how rich people live and by experiencing vicariously the feeling of infinite and unlimited riches.

# OPEN THE COSMIC STOREHOUSE OF RICHES AND OBTAIN AN UNLIMITED SUPPLY OF MONEY

# 9

There is a great cosmic storehouse of riches that exists in the invisible world of vibration. In this storehouse there are all the treasures that have been created for man to use and enjoy.

This cosmic storehouse of riches may be tapped by any person who knows a few cosmic principles regarding the secret laws of life.

You can obtain unlimited supplies of money once you know its basic vibratory rate. Everything in the universe operates under this invisible law of vibration, as illustrated by Pythagoras, when he proved that all matter is nothing more nor less than invisible masses of atoms that vibrate in different wavelengths or rhythms.

Scientists say that if one could obtain the rate of vibration of a bridge, such as the Brooklyn Bridge, and play that note on a giant violin, it could shatter the bridge to pieces!

The noted tenor Caruso used to prove this theory of vibration at dinner parties. He would obtain the basic rhythm of a glass tumbler by running his finger over the rim when it was dampened. When he found out the note it gave off, he would sing that note into the glass and shatter it to bits.

Your mind is able to trigger this cosmic vibratory mass of spiritual energy and cause it to release for your benefit money or the equivalents of money—possessions, houses, lands, cars, home furnishings, stocks, jewels, or furs. Anything that has a money value has its equivalent vibration in your mind, and can be invoked by using this cosmic regimen.

Just as a computer can be programmed to release certain data that has been programmed into it by pressing a few keys, so too, your higher mind can be programmed with cosmic images of money or its equivalents, and trigger instant reaction in the world of vibration.

A house, tree, or human being is nothing more nor less than billions of these invisible atoms, gathered together and held together by the invisible cosmic rhythm of creation. The creative command given in the Bible, "Let there be light," was the command that sent the atoms hurtling out into space to create the billions of worlds that exist in the infinity of time and space.

Everywhere you look in nature you see this cosmic law at work. In the invisible interstices of the universe there exists the pattern that can create a field of wheat, a red rose, or another human being. This cosmic law of duplication is in the seed of the species that is to be created. The creative command goes out in the invisible universe and assembles the atoms and molecules to create anything that you desire in your universe.

Just as the Empire State Building had its invisible form in the mind of Al Smith, who thought of the idea, and the architect who drew up the plans for the building of the giant skyscraper, so too your mind must form the concepts of those things which money can buy, and release these images to the architect of the universe to create money or its equivalents in your own life.

## REGIMEN TO OPEN
## THE COSMIC STOREHOUSE OF RICHES

1. Program your higher mind with creative commands that will start the flow of spiritual energy in the invisible universe. The first of these creative commands is: "I desire money and its equivalents to do the things I want to do in life." Repeat this statement five times, as you sit in meditation.

2. Write down the things you want this higher power to bring you, so you will have specific things programmed into your higher consciousness.

These desires can be stated as follows, using your own specific desires for things you want. The following is only an example:

I desire a new car for my family's and my benefit.

I desire a new apartment (or house) located in the country.

I desire the sum of $5,000 to pay up all my bills and give me feelings of security for the future.

I desire a business of my own. (Here state nature of the business.)

I desire jewlery, tape recorders, a color TV set, a refrigerator, washing machine and dryer, household furnishings to make my life more comfortable, and give me a few luxuries.

I desire travel for cultural purposes and for adventure.

3. After you have written these desires down, read them over carefully and keep the sheet of paper where you can see it at least two or three times a day. Read it over at night, just before going to sleep so your subconscious mind will become imprinted with this creative command. Then again, when you arise in the morning, read it over and repeat it as many times during the day as you can think of it.

4. Sit for 15 minutes daily and concentrate the power of your mind on methods by which you might obtain money or its

equivalents. Run through your higher mind centers pictures of
yourself receiving money through the mail; see yourself getting
a bonus at your place of business; mentally visualize yourself
getting an income tax refund.

A man who used this method of cosmic programming for
money kept visualizing himself getting money in letters. He
mentally projected the thought that people would send him
money through the mails, but he did not know for what object.
One day he saw a small ad telling him he could start his own
mail order business for a few hundred dollars. He sent for the
information and just two months later, he ran across an item he
could import from Germany, which every woman would want
in her kitchen. He placed small ads in various magazines and
soon orders were pouring in by mail! The first month of
business he opened letters and took out $2,000 in checks,
money orders and cash. His subconscious mind had programmed a method for him to grow rich, which fit his exact
requirements.

5. When you have tested this power in small ways and
begin the flow of money or its equivalents, you can expand
your thinking into higher brackets of income. Sit quietly and
program your higher mind with this statement:

> I now magnetize my higher mind centers with bigger concepts
> of money and supply. I project the following vibrations to
> trigger the cosmic jackpot of gold.

6. When you have stated this cosmic programming command, write down on a sheet of paper the following:

> I now magnetize the sum of $1,000.
> I now magnetize the sum of $5,000.
> I now magnetize the sum of $10,000.

7. You may not receive the $1,000 all at once, but you
may get a check for $100 from an unexpected source. Keep

track of this in a little book which you can call My Cosmic Bank Book. Write down "Received the sum of $100."

Another day you might get a gift worth $10. Write this down in your Cosmic Bank Book also.

Someone may invite you to dinner, or the theater, and easily spend 25 or 30 dollars. This is also money or its equivalents, so enter this in your cosmic bookkeeping.

Everytime someone gives you something of value, or you make extra money from some unexpected source, add it to your account, and at the end of each month balance your books and see if you have not received the equivalent of your first $1,000.

A woman who tried this system put down that she and her husband wanted the sum of $1,000 within a month. They kept track of the various amounts they received and found that within the month the following unexpected things had happened to them.

The husband got a weekly raise of $10 in salary, which in one year amounted to $520. The wife had wanted a piano for some time, but they felt they could not afford one. Two weeks after starting this system of cosmic bookkeeping, a friend was moving from her apartment and offered her an upright piano, old but still extremely good, if she would pay for the moving of it! This was easily worth $300.

Two separate items came a week from each other; a prize was being given by her club, a color TV set for the lucky number drawn. She won it! That was another $500 added to their cosmic account. They had already attracted more than $1,000 by this system of cosmic programming of money or its equivalents!

8. To build money awareness and enrich your consciousness, project mental pictures of the things you want to the cosmic mind. This helps trigger invisible atomic vibrations in the vast computer of the universe, and starts to assemble the invisible spiritual protoplasm to bring you the things you desire. To help you do this with more realism, get a Sears Roebuck

Catalogue, or any catalogue of a mail order house like Montgomery Ward, or Spiegel, and mentally order the objects that you want from this catalogue. This cosmic window shopping helps crystallize the mind with the images of the things you want money to buy. As money is only frozen energy of your mind, this exercise will help unlock the mystical power of your higher mind to show you how to get the money to purchase the things you put down in your mental catalogue.

A woman in our lecture work used this system to open the cosmic storehouse of riches with a catalogue. She mentally ordered a beautiful fur coat worth $575. She filled out her order blank for a new refrigerator, a new bedroom suite, and a color TV set.

These things did not come to her all at once, but within two weeks from the time she began her practice of this law she was given a beautiful mink coat that had cost her mother-in-law $1,500. As the woman was moving from New York to Florida, she felt she would no longer need it, so she gave it to her daughter-in-law!

Her husband was a carpenter, and one day he offered to help their next door neighbor do a little remodeling of a playroom for their two children. The man spent three weekends doing the work and at the end of that time the owner of the house asked him how much he owed him for his carpentry work. The man replied, "Nothing. Someday you can probably help me and my wife out with something."

Two days later, a $1,200 Zenith color TV set was delivered at their door! The neighbors had purchased a new set, and gave this excellent, two-year-old set to the carpenter and his wife!

Each of the items on her Cosmic Catalogue list appeared as mysteriously in that year, until she had everything she had mentally projected onto the invisible mental and spiritual plane.

### POINTS TO REMEMBER

1. Tap the unlimited supplies of money once you learn

the basic vibratory rate of money in the invisible universe.

2. Your mind can trigger the cosmic vibratory mass of spiritual energy in the invisible cosmos and make it release money, houses, lands, cars, furnishings, stocks, jewels and furs for your benefit and enrichment.

3. The cosmic law of duplication can create anything you image in your mind.

4. The creative command "I desire money" can be used to bring you unlimited riches.

5. Program your desires into your higher mind and start the flow of cosmic energy to produce your desires in tangible form, including money, houses, lands and other valuables.

6. A man used this system to build a mail order business that began bringing him in $2,000 a month at once.

7. Magnetize sums ranging from $1,000 to $10,000 in a simple way by using cosmic programming commands to your higher mind.

8. Draw on your Cosmic Bank Book for various sums of money and attract money or its equivalents immediately.

9. A woman received a piano within two weeks after starting this system of cosmic bookkeeping. A color TV set came a short time later, and her husband got a $520 raise a year in salary.

10. To build money awareness, start to order from a Cosmic Catalogue the things you want and this will trigger instant reactions.

11. A woman used this system and triggered a beautiful fur coat that had cost $1,500. A short time later she was able to attract a $1,200 Zenith TV set and other valuable items.

# 10 POSITIVE STEPS UP THE GOLDEN STAIRWAY TO YOUR DESIRED FORTUNE

# 10

In the lives of more than 10,000 successful men and women I have studied, I found that each used the following 10 positive steps up the golden stairway to their desired fortunes. Consciously or subconsciously, these people were guided up that golden ladder of dreams that leads to fame and fortune. You too can follow in their inspired footsteps and automatically achieve your desired goals of money, power, social prestige, love fulfillment, intellectual triumphs and financial security for your family and yourself.

Money magnetism can be built by constant concentration and practice. Each day invoke one or more of these 10 positive forces to magnetize your mind and direct you up that golden ladder of dreams which brings success and fulfillment.

### Step No. 1: Emotionalized desires

You probably have often said, "If I only had a million dollars, I could do anything I want in life."

This is a desire and when you express it casually, it has little effect on you or your destiny.

However, if you think or say, with emotional intensity, "I need money to pay off my mortgage and give security to my family," or "I want money so I can give my children an education," or "I would like money to be able to buy a comfortable home for my family," you are invoking the power of emotionalized desire.

The emotions have been given to man to be used for power to accelerate the mind's and body's normal functions. Every time you emotionalize your desires and think a thought with intensity, it instantly sets up reactions in your autonomic nervous system and triggers glandular reactions that give you the physical power to achieve that which you desire.

The emotionalized desire of man to fly like a bird led to our stupendous achievements in creating the airplane and reaching out to the very stars in our quest for new horizons.

The desire to communicate over long distances led Marconi and Alexander Graham Bell to invent the wireless and the telephone.

The desire to find new worlds led Columbus on his perilous voyages of discovery.

The desire to give humanity new sources of power and energy led to the splitting of the atom.

Always, back of every great achievement, there is this tremendous force of emotionalized desire.

Repeat each day for at least a month, until you have built habits of thinking in terms of emotional desire, the thoughts you wish to express about the things you want in life.

I desire money to educate my children.

I desire fame and fortune so I can better serve the world.

I desire to invent an object that can benefit humanity and also make me rich.

I desire intellectual knowledge to better create something of enduring value.

I desire my own business, so I can give better products and services to the world and also accumulate money to build security for my family in the future.

I desire the creative talents of writing, painting, composing, chemical discoveries, inventing, (or any other talent you wish to develop) so I may bring beauty and good to humanity.

## Step No. 2: Creative imagination

When man first discovered gold in the earth, in ancient times, it meant no more to him than rocks or other metal. It was only when someone, through his imagination, began to visualize using the shiny, gold metal for ornaments, jewelry and adornment, that gold became valuable.

When primitive man lived in caves, there were trees all around, but no one had the creative imagination to visualize building a home from the branches. First, someone had to have the imagination to visualize a stone or metal axe, with which to cut down the trees from which to build a home.

Your creative imagination is one of the most important positive steps to take you up the golden stairway to your desired fortune.

Each day, for 15 minutes a day, exercise the power of your creative imagination by doing the following exercises:

Imagine yourself writing a story; plot it, think up the characters from everyday people you know. Write down a short synopsis of what the characters are going to do. From this simple script, you may evolve a story that can bring enjoyment to millions of people and also bring you a fortune.

Go into the area of your imagination to expand your creative powers. As another mental exercise, sit quietly for a few moments and imagine what it would be like to receive $100,000 from a lottery ticket, even if they do not have lotteries in your state, this is only a mental exercise. See yourself going on a shopping spree, buying all the beautiful things you have long dreamed of. What would you buy first? A new car? A color TV set? A down payment on a home of your own or new furnishings for your apartment or house? Run the pictures of what you would do with the money through your imagination. This stirs the creative faculties and causes them to release ideas of how you can make that money to obtain the things you desire.

### Step No. 3: Have faith in yourself and your talents

Faith is a miracle-working power. If you believe that you can make a big success you will be able to summon up the powers to achieve its accomplishment:

- Faith in selling things by mail made a fortune for Sears Roebuck.
- Faith in rubber built the Goodrich and Goodyear empires.
- Faith in healing drugs created the Ligget Drug stores.
- Faith in the power to beautify women with her products led to Helena Rubenstein's success in the field of cosmetics.

To increase your faith in yourself and your talents, program your subconscious mind with the following positive statements:

I have faith that I can achieve a great destiny.
I believe I can own my own business and make $50,000 a year
or more.
I have faith that the $5,000 will come to pay off my debts.
I believe I have hidden potentials for greatness and I now
overcome all feelings of inadequacy and inferiority

Repeat these positive programming statements just before you go to sleep at night. Say the ones that fit your needs several times and feel, with positive emotion, the full impact of what you are programming.

A man who was in the educational system in Philadelphia

heard that they were trying to find a new supervisor of schools in New York City about 15 years ago. The job paid a salary of $35,000 year, which was excellent in those days. He applied for the job and received it. Other educators in New York City, who were as highly trained as he was, complained bitterly that he had won the job and they hadn't. The simple fact of the matter was that not one of those involved in New York City had faith in himself and *no one had actually applied for the job!* It went to an out-of-town educator who had faith in himself and his abilities.

### Step No. 4: Have tremendous enthusiasm for whatever you are doing

In a recent television program on the lives of the four Rockefeller brothers, one of them remarked that if a person likes his work and enjoys doing it, he can become successful.

Do you face your day's work with enthusiasm and joy? If not, then it is not your life's work and you will never become rich through your job. If you can do so without incurring financial problems, give it up and get into work you really enjoy and can be enthusiastic about.

### Step No. 5: Develop curiosity about life and the things that could make your life more productive and interesting

Curiosity has led to many great discoveries throughout history. Burbank was curious to know what would happen if he grafted slips from orange, lemon and grapefruit trees on one citrus tree. He discovered the tree would bear all three species of fruit. From this discovery came all his discoveries in the field of horticulture that produced improved strains of fruits and vegetables that have benefited all mankind.

Benjamin Franklin was curious to know what would happen if he sent a kite up into an electrical storm with a key attached to the string. From this came the harnessing of electricity to drive man's motors and bring into being our great industrial age.

Study the lives of people like Galileo, Columbus, Michelangelo, Leonardo da Vinci, Pasteur, Edison, Burbank, Rockefeller, Morgan, Vanderbilt, Onassis, J. Paul Getty, and others in past ages and in our own modern age, who have achieved greatness and made fortunes and discover the secrets they used to amass wealth.

**Step No. 6. Have the courage to dream big and dare to achieve more than ordinary people do**

Cecil Rhodes, who founded the Rhodes Scholarship, was a tubercular, given up by the doctors when he was a young man. He had the courage to leave England and go to unexplored Africa to regain his health. Without money and without help from a living soul, he began to carve an empire for himself out of that vast continent. Not only did he regain his health, but he soon discovered a diamond field that made him rich. Then he began to buy up hundreds of thousands of acreas of land, and he planted 50,000 trees on his vast estate, which included a gigantic mountain and a lake. He said of wealth, "No one should think in terms of a dozen of anything; he should think in terms of thousands, millions. Only in this way can he achieve the big things he dreams of."

Dare to dream big! Have a concept of owning your own home, of buying land that will make you wealthy in the future.

Write down on a piece of paper the sum of $1,000,000 and on it these words: "I now build my consciousness to conceive of big things, a big fortune, a great destiny. I project the sum of $1,000,000 in my future." Keep this paper where you can look at it two or three times a day, until its programming is stamped upon your subconscious mind. You do not need $1,000,000 to be financially secure or happy, but holding this big sum in consciousness makes it possible for you to achieve varying amounts, that will give you complete security for the future.

Step No. 7: Exercise your will to succeed daily

Set small daily goals that you can fulfill, such as writing letters, thinking of new projects, interviewing prospective employers, learning a new word, studying a foreign language, starting a novel, a poem, or a song—anything that you feel will exercise this will to succeed. Your will is like a muscle; the more you exercise it the stronger it grows.

There is a will to live, a will to succeed, a will to love, a will to power, a will to social reciprocity. These are mental forces that must be daily exercised to overcome the opposite polarity of failure, sickness, weakness, and loneliness. The will to fail is so strong in most people that it influences their every act in life.

To overcome this negative magnetic force, exercise the will to succeed each day by doing something that takes an act of will. If you smoke and wish you didn't, make it a habit to smoke a little less each day. If you spend too much money, force yourself to go without spending any that entire day. If you waste time by watching too much television, force yourself to spend an hour of your time doing something for self-improvement.

Step No. 8: Use your time and energy wisely and carefully, for time is the golden substance of life and money.

You have only 24 precious hours daily. Eight hours are for work; eight hours for sleep; this takes up 16 golden hours a day. You have eight precious hours left to spend as you wish. Entertainment, television viewing, and social activities may take up four of these golden hours. You still have four hours left in which to develop your mind, study a course that will prepare you for a new occupation or to concentrate on methods for increasing your income.

I was once on a plane going to Athens, Greece, and sat next to a young man about 25 years of age. During that long flight of about 11 hours, I noticed that he had a briefcase at his feet, filled with various types of books. I peeked over his shoulders while he studied these books intently. Finally I talked to him, and discovered that he was preparing himself for a teaching job at the University of Athens. He had kept up this method of study for several years while he educated himself and at the same time, kept a full-time job. He crowded his education into evening courses at a university in New York, and now he was eligible for a teaching position at that early age!

This young man will achieve his life goal through his wise use of his time and energy. He planned his life so there were few wasted moments in it, and I knew that he was on the way to complete goal achievement.

If your education was interrupted, don't use it as an excuse for failure. There are excellent night schools that cost nothing but your time and energy; attend these and study any course you wish.

I know a very excellent woman artist in New York City who started taking an evening course at the Art Student's League, where she paid a modest tuition. In two year's time this woman was doing fashion designing for a very prominent dress manufacturer, and making a very good salary.

### Step No. 9: Practice being generous and unselfish

The hand, or heart, or mind that is closed never gives anything to the world, but neither can it receive anything. To obtain maximum benefits in life and truly magnetize your mind centers with money awareness, adopt a generous attitude toward life. Don't be penny-pinching and miserly. It's good to build habits of thrift and saving, but don't let them degenerate into scrimping and denying yourself the good things of life.

A woman who came to my lectures in California told me once that she had been saving a purple silk dress for 35 years so she would have something beautiful in which to be buried! After coming to a few of our lectures, she learned that one must not live for such events but utilize everything one has, get rid of things one doesn't need, and by creating a vacuum nature rushes in to fill it with something else of value.

She told me that she went home one night, after a class, and decided to take out the purple dress and begin to wear it. When she unfolded the tissue paper in which it was wrapped, the beautiful silk dress fell apart where it had been creased all those years in her bureau drawer!

Practice giving something away daily. It doesn't have to be money or anything of intrinsic value. Give better service in your job. Give smiles of encouragement to those who are discouraged Give praise and kindness and consideration. Give love when someone does something for you. And if you can give to some worthy charity, your local church, or community chest, give something of your substance and your own good will be increased. This law of giving is in the Bible, where it says, "Give, and it shall be given unto you, good measure, pressed down and running over. For with what measure you mete withal it shall be measured unto you."

### Step No. 10: Take dynamic action to achieve your dream

Action is the first law of the universe. You can sit and daydream all your life that you will have a fortune and that you will be famous and successful, but if you do not take that first step through dynamic action, it is doubtful that you will get anywhere.

There is a saying from ancient China, "A journey of a thousand miles begins with but a single step."

Take that first step today to achieve your dreams of fame and fortune. If you want to write a great novel, don't expect to do it in one day or one month, but begin with a sheet of paper on which you write your title and a few beginning words. Your subconscious mind will soon come through to help you and every time you sit down to write; this power will take over and shape your sentences and write for you.

Ernest Hemingway programmed his subconscious mind to write only 500 words a day on whatever book he was working. He would sit down at his desk at six in the morning and stay there until those 500 words were finished. Then he would do other things for the balance of the day. In this way he accomplished more than most writers who sit down occasionally and then let other things interfere with their writing.

Do the same thing if you want to paint great pictures, or invent some object, or compose a beautiful song: sit down and go into meditation, letting your mind rove over the many possibilities, until you select a theme for your work; then let your subconscious mind take over the actual work. Form a daily habit of facing your creative tasks every day at the same time.

If you want to magnetize your mind for more money, give some time daily to studying things relating to money.

## POINTS TO REMEMBER

1. Use the emotion of desire to magnetize money and achieve a great destiny.
2. The great achievements of history were achieved through emotionalized desire.
3. The six creative and magnetic statements program into your subconscious mind fame, power and riches.
4. Remember the vital importance of building a creative imagination to shape the future destiny and attract money, houses, lands, jewelry and other possessions.
5. Use the dynamic power of faith to magnetize your mind centers with concepts of wealth and success.
6. The power of enthusiasm releases creative energy for building a fortune and achieving your desired goals.
7. Dare to dream big to achieve the great destiny you desire.

8. Develop your will to succeed.
9. Utilize the precious gold of time for achieving money.
10. A young man I met on a plane going to Athens changed his entire life by utilizing his time constructively.
11. Be generous and unselfish in your drive to fame and fortune.
12. Take dynamic action and begin now to do the great things you desire.

# THE MILLION-DOLLAR
# PERSONALITY THAT
# MAGNETIZES YOUR AURA
# WITH MONEY KNOW-HOW

# 11

You can build a magnetic aura of power and success in your personality that will actually attract money to you like a magnet!

People who have achieved great fortunes first had to build a million-dollar personality with money know-how. You've heard the sayings "Money talks"; "Nothing succeeds like success"; "Money goes to money"; "Show me a man's friends and I will tell you what his character is like." These sayings all relate to the great magnetic law of attraction. When you magnetize your aura with money know-how, you will be invoking one of the great universal laws for achieving a fortune.

If you build an aura of failure, lack of confidence and poverty, other people instantly sense this and run from you. People like to help those who have an air of self-confidence, poise and power.

Money magnetism begins in your mind first; here it is that

you create the aura that surrounds you and becomes the outer expression of your inner personality.

Psychologists now say that children who become successful in life usually had parents who built their confidence and sense of self-importance by appreciating the child's efforts, by praising and encouraging him, and by giving the child self-confidence. They say this occurs in the child's development by the time he has reached the age of 10.

If the parents have built an aura of failure, discouragement, and negativity in the child's personality, these children seldom achieve success in life. Of course, this negative aura can be broken by showing a person how to overcome the effects of such disastrous programming.

In this chapter you will learn how to build the million-dollar personality so you can magnetize money with your aura and attract everything you desire in life.

## REGIMEN FOR BUILDING
## THE MILLION-DOLLAR PERSONALITY

1. Mentally change your self-image from one of failure, poverty and negativity to one of confidence, importance and success. How can you do this? By programming yourself every day just before you go out to meet the challenges of life.

To do this, stand before your mirror and say the following positive programming statements:

I now build my magic circle aura of importance and success. I shall conquer everyone I meet today with the projection of charm, poise and magnetism. I now have a sense of money awareness; I am worth $50,000 a year, or more, and I now project this image of riches, power, fame and creativity to every person I meet today.

2. Now mentally visualize that you are wearing an invisible crown. Lift your head high, hold your chin up, and keep your

spine straight. A crown cannot be held on a head that is bent forward in dejection, fear and negativity. Look the world in the eye, and know that your invisible crown gives you authority, power and magnetism. Others will sense it when you adopt this posture of command and control.

3. Now say to yourself, or aloud, the following positive statements:

> I was born to rule and command the forces of life. I now reign over the hearts and minds of people with the projection of love and kindness. I want to help others, and in turn, they will want to help me. I shall project this sense of love all day today to everyone I meet.

4. Now you are ready to clear your subconscious mind of all the negative programming that you have built into your personality over the years. Say this positive statement:

> I now break the mold of past negativity. I overcome fear with confidence. I build a sense of success and money power, knowing that I have the gifts and talents that can make me a money magnet. I overcome all negative forces from my early childhood and believe in myself and my talents. I know I can sell my product to every customer I approach today. I know I can make a fortune, using my money know-how. I magnetize my aura with success, riches and power and I attract these elements in my life here and now.

I once gave this secret of money know-how to a used-car salesman in Philadelphia. He had been having a hard time selling cars, and the moment I met him at one of my lectures, I knew why. He approached each customer with a feeling that they were only looking and that they were not really interested in buying a car. This attitude showed in his shifty gaze, his ambling walk, his whining, complaining voice. He said, "I think each customer hates me. They challenge everything I say about the car and don't believe me."

I then explained to him that his personality reflected these elements of suspicion and lack of confidence. His customers were only mirroring his mental attitude.

I gave this man the regimen for building his aura with more magnetism and within the week he came back and told me he had averaged selling four cars a day! His entire personality had changed from a negative one to a bright, positive and magnetic one that made him a money magnet.

5. To build your magnetic aura in what I call the magic circle, stand before your mirror again and spread out your arms to your sides. Now turn around a few times and say:

> This is my magic circle kingdom, over which I rule. This aura I now fill with the golden light of my presence. I rule over this kingdom with kindness, gentility, beauty and love. I fill my invisible kindgom with magnetism and power. It becomes a magnet attracting into my orbit of life successful people, who will help me achieve my life goal

6. Now mentally visualize this aura, which is your little world, over which you reign as a king or queen, being filled with golden light. Gold is the symbol of wealth and power. You and you alone have power to control what happens in your own little personal world. You can build it with an aura of optimism, charm and beauty, or you can make it a dark, dismal prison house of fear, failure and frustration. Whenever you feel a sense of negativity, mentally see your magic circle filled with golden light. Light banishes darkness. You will now concentrate on the following forces that you will put into your magic circle aura; these represent the light, not the darkness. You can think or say the following statements:

> I now magnetize my magic circle with beauty. I think thoughts of beauty and they reflect in my facial expression, in my words, and in the way I clothe myself, wear my hair, and the way I speak.

I magnetize my magic circle with peace and I radiate peace and tranquility in my aura.

I now project in my magic circle the quality of optimism and good cheer. I believe things are getting better, not worse. I see people as being honest, not dishonest. I change my thinking regarding money; it is easy to attract, not difficult. All rich people are *not* crooks, and money is *not* evil, but good.

I now magnetize my mind centers and my magic circle aura with money-power, knowing that I shall attract all the money I need for everything I desire in my life.

I once gave this magic circle aura to a young girl who came to Hollywood to become a movie star. She had a burning desire to be famous, but she felt she was too plain and too angular and not talented enough. I put her on a circular platform, dressed her in a purple robe, put a crown on her head and gave her a scepter to carry. I then gave her the full magic circle royalty treatment. This girl changed her entire personality within a few weeks time, with constant practice. She was given a screen test by M.G.M. and went on to become one of their biggest stars!

I have given this magic circle to such stars as Claudette Colbert, Gloria Swanson, Bette Davis, Loretta Young, Bob Hope, Robert Taylor, Tyrone Power, Clark Gable, Joan Crawford, Nelson Eddy, William Holden, Spencer Tracy, Greer Garson, and about 200 other famous stars, and each of them went on to fame and fortune. I had pictures taken with these stars when they were young, and they were published in movie magazines, living proof that my system of the magic circle can work for anyone who seriously uses it. You may not become a movie star, but you will be a star on the stage of your own life, and you will magnetize fame, fortune, and all the money you need to be happy in the future.

When Napoleon was a soldier on the battlefields of France, he made the decision that he would one day become the Emperor of France. But he was only a little over five feet tall, and did not look, talk or act like an Emperor. He called in one of the great tragedians of that day named Talma, and said to him, "Show me how to act the part of an Emperor." The great actor made Napoleon stand before a full-length mirror; he put a book on his head and said, "Visualize that is your crown." Then he gave him a stick to hold in his hand, "Think of this as your royal scepter. Now walk back and forth and say aloud, 'I am Emperor Napoleon the First.' "

Talma gave Napoleon his magic circle of power and command. Later, when Napoleon crowned himself Emperor Napoleon Bonaparte the First, the crowned heads of Europe bowed before his power and his might. He had successfully built his magic circle of greatness.

In building your aura with the magic circle principles, do not let them degenerate into arrogance, ego or dominance. The magic circle magnetizes your outer personality with the inner qualities and these should be kindness, gentility, beauty, peace, love, generosity, tolerance, humility, faith, good, and a sense of value. The world will recognize these positive elements in your aura and they will rush to reward you with friendship, love, money and things of value.

## POINTS TO REMEMBER

1. You can build a magnetic aura through the million-dollar personality that attracts money to you like a magnet.
2. Change your self-image from one of failure and poverty to one of confidence and success through a programming regimen that gives your aura a money know-how.
3. Create the magic circle aura of importance and success that brings you money awareness and power to demonstrate all the money you require.
4. Clear your subconscious mind of all past negative programmings of failure, poverty and unhappiness; and

replace it with an aura of confidence, power, riches and abundance.

5. A used-car salesman in Philadelphia used this magnetic money know-how, and began to sell four cars a day, when formerly he seldom sold any.

6. Your magic circle aura can be magentized with love, beauty, peace, money or any other quality that you want to attract in your life.

7. A young actress in Hollywood, to whom I gave this magic circle of power, went on to become one of Hollywood's brightest stars.

8. Movie stars Gloria Swanson, Claudette Colbert, Bette Davis, Loretta Young, Bob Hope, Joan Crawford, Greer Garson, and hundreds of others to whom I gave the Magic Circle use this magnetic principle to bring them fame and fortune.

9. The secret power of the magic circle was used by Napoleon Bonaparte when he became the Emperor of France.

10. You can create an aura of kindness, gentility, beauty, generosity, richness, faith and good that will surround you like a magic circle and charm people as well as magnetize and attract money into your life orbit.

# THE PSYCHIC WHIRLPOOL
# OF MONEY CAN BRING YOU
# RICHES AND ABUNDANCE

# 12

There is a psychic power within your higher mind which you can motivate to guide you to fame, fortune and success. You can create a psychic whirlpool of money within these higher mind centers that will guide you unerringly to riches. This psychic guidance has led many people to success.

Jesse Livermore once got a psychic hunch to sell Southern Pacific railroad stocks short. He had put all his money into the accumulation of this stock. A few days later the San Francisco earthquake came and the stock plummeted more than 100 points overnight. Livermore became a millionaire by playing this psychic hunch.

You can create a psychic whirlpool of infinite riches and abundance in your own life. You can learn how to be guided by your higher psychic mind centers to achieve fame, fortune and success. You can tap the higher mind that exists within every person, and be shown how to make your money magnet attract for you any sum from $1,000 to $1,000,000.

In this chapter we shall learn this method for building your psychic money awareness, so there will not be so much effort on your part. Many people struggle for a lifetime and never achieve financial security. It is estimated that 95 percent of all people who reach the age of 65 lose their fortunes and are dependent on relatives or welfare.

I once did research for a book I was writing called *The Million Dollar Secret that Lies Hidden Within Your Mind.* I checked on the lives of 12 people who had won $100,000 or more in the Irish Sweepstakes. Out of the 12, nine lost their money within two to three years, and only three were able to build financial security!

### REGIMEN TO BUILD YOUR PSYCHIC WHIRLPOOL FOR INFINITE RICHES AND ABUNDANCE

**1. Your higher psychic centers can guide you to the source of your riches and abundance if you train them daily.**
To train your psychic centers, sit quietly in meditation for 15 minutes a day. Repeat the following words silently, as you program this higher psychic center with directions for enriching your life.

> I now program my higher mind with a desire to become successful and rich. I ask for psychic guidance to the right field of endeavor to achieve my goal of financial security and independence. I wish to be told the following things:
>> What business should I go into to become rich?
>> What product should I sell?
>> How can I get someone with money to back me in business?
>> What creative talents do I have that can make me rich?
>> Where can I get the money I need to go into business?
>> Who should I take into partnership with me?

When you have stated these psychic stimulators, sit back confidently and let whatever thoughts come to your mind flow, without making any effort to think. Sometimes an idea will come to you in the first session that can bring you success. At other times nothing will come through. In such cases, go about your regular daily activities and your higher psychic centers will be at work on your problem, assembling facts from your subconscious mind for your money success.

Sometimes you will be led to do something that brings you into the very situation you needed to bring you the success you asked for, as was the case with a student of mine, who asked for the sum of $5,000 to meet her financial needs at once. She had lost her husband and had two small children to take care of. She had only one special talent; she was a very good cook and baker and kept a beautiful home. Other than that she had no special training in business or money making.

She went into her psychic session each day for a week, and nothing seemed to come through. But one day she was reading a woman's magazine when she saw a full page contest offering big prizes for the best cake recipe made from the advertiser's flour. This rang a bell in this woman's higher psychic centers, and something told her to enter the contest.

She later told me that while she was mixing her cake, putting in the ingredients and baking it, she felt a sense of exhilaration and confidence that she was going to win the first prize, which happened to be $5,000.

When the prizes were announced this woman was notified that her cake had won the first prize of $5,000! This was the exact amount she had asked for.

2. **To create a psychic whirlpool, sit in meditation and visualize an actual whirlpool.** This occurs when a stream of water pours down from a great height and starts to rotate round and round, sucking everything on the outer periphery of the whirlpool down into the center. There is such a natural whirlpool at the bottom of Niagra Falls, and when you go down to the bottom of the Falls on the Maid of the Mist, a ship that carries passengers under the falls, you can see this gigantic whirlpool pulling everything towards its center.

Now, when you sit quietly in your next meditation, visualize your mind being like that whirlpool. On the outer periphery you will see all the things that you want to do with money. You want to buy your own home, you want beautiful furnishings, you desire a color television set, a refrigerator, the most modern vacuum cleaner, washing machine and dryer, a new car, beautiful jewelry and fine clothing. All these things that money represents are there, on the outer circumference of your experiences.

Now mentally begin to pull in to the center of the psychic whirlpool each of the things that you want to attract. Take one thing at a time, and let your desires and emotions swell to a pitch of emotional intensity. As you select each thing you want your higher psychic centers to demonstrate for you, close your eyes and say the following mystical incantation to magnetize the object:

I now magnetize my psychic whirlpool through the emotion of desire. I attract into the innermost core of my being the beautiful concept of a home that I shall one day own. I see it furnished beautifully. I see myself entertaining my friends in it. I see the small garden, the beautiful trees surrounding it. I walk through the six rooms admiring the furnishings. I see my family living in our dream home in the future and I now claim this psychic dream as my own.

3. **When you have used this meditation of the psychic whirlpool for one object, rest a while and do the next meditation on the following day.** This time you might select a car that you want money for. Sit quietly in a place where you will not be disturbed for at least half an hour. Now mentally visualize a new car, the model, make and color that you desire. Close your eyes for this psychic whirlpool exercise. Now repeat these words, or make up those you want to use.

I now project through my psychic whirlpool the mental picture of the car I wish to own and drive. I see the Chevrolet,

four door sedan, blue color and red upholstery, and I project
my family and myself riding in the car, visiting friends, taking
trips on picnics and visits in the country. I now invoke the law
of psychic dominance to bring this car from the outer
periphery of the world into the inner, subjective world of
reality.

To show you how this psychic whirlpool creates the
invisible magnetic force that draws things into your orbit of
experience, let me tell you of the example of two students of
mine, a husband and wife, who projected their desires through
the psychic whirlpool and attracted amazing things.

They wrote in a recent letter to me, "Since attending your
lectures and learning the law of the psychic whirlpool, we have
received the sums of $1,000, $5,000, $10,000 and $20,000; and
also a white Fleetwood Cadillac." Then the letter goes on to tell
of other miraculous things that happened to a sick mother who
was healed and moved into a new location.

You may invoke this psychic whirlpool for anything you
desire in life. If you want that dream home, realize that the
lumber is somewhere in a forest, ready to build your home. If
you want a piano for your living room, know that somewhere in
a showroom this beautiful instrument is waiting to be drawn
into the magnetic whirlpool of your desires and aspirations.

Another student of mine in New York City had a desire
for an upright piano. She was a music teacher and had come to
New York City from the Midwest. She attended a recital where
music students were being presented by a conservatory of
music. She had no money with which to buy a piano; in fact,
she did not have employment at the time, and her savings were
running short. There at the recital she met a man who ran the
conservatory and when he learned she was a music teacher, he
offered her a job at the music school.

In her first week of teaching, she noticed that an upright
piano was kept stored in a basement room. She inquired about
it, and found it had been there some years and was not actually
needed. She made an offer for it and was told a ridiculously low

price. She offered to buy it and paid a small sum weekly out of her salary for its purchase. She now had her piano and was able to build her own personal clientele in her apartment, making as much money in her spare time as she did at her job!

**4. If you want the psychic whirlpool to bring you specific sums of money, sit in meditation and visualize that money already in existence somewhere in the world.** See it stored in bank vaults—fresh, crisp $20, $50, and $100 bills just waiting to be drawn into someone's magnetic whirlpool.

Now project in your mind's psychic center the sum of money you want and create a magnetic desire for it, knowing what you want the money for. Say the following words to yourself:

> I now draw into my psychic whirlpool the sum that I need to pay off my mortgage. I ask for guidance as to how I can attract this money and I now await instructions from my higher psychic mind centers.

A young man who came to my classes in New York City had a desire to attract more money so he could buy a restaurant. He worked as a waiter and had saved some money but not nearly enough to buy anything worthwhile.

When he learned how to create the psychic whirlpool of infinite riches and abundance, he was guided to quit his job as a waiter and he obtained a job as a messenger in a big stock brokerage firm. He delivered securities from one office to the other of this large company, and also very confidential reports on the stocks that clients were to buy or sell. He kept studying these reports in his spare time, and he saw that the recommended stocks invariably went up, and the brokers bought thousands of shares for their clients, whereas the stocks that were given a negative report always seemed to go down.

One day he saw a confidential report about a stock that

was selling for $2 a share. He had saved $2,000 so he bought 1,000 shares of this stock and waited for results.

Within a period of four months this stock soared to $22 a share, and he sold his 1,000 shares, making a profit of nearly $20,000 after paying the broker's fees! He immediately quit his job as a delivery boy and began to look for a place he could rent for a restaurant. He found an ideal corner location, and opened a small coffee shop. Now, five years later, this young man has three bigger restaurants and is well on the way to making his first million!

**5. The bigger sums of money require a great deal more concentration and psychic motivation.** If you want $50,000 to educate your children, buy a home of your own, or to go into some big business, sit in meditation and visualize in the whirlpool of money $1,000 bills whirling round and round. See yourself as a syphon, sucking into the core of your magnetism the $1,000 bills. Count them and see yourself receiving them, banking them and spending them. Then ask your higher psychic mind centers how you can get this $50,000. Use this magnetic statement:

> I now desire the sum of $50,000 to buy a home, to help educate my children. I want to magnetize and attract this large sum to give me security for the future. Give me an idea or guide me to a business investment that can open wide the doors to the storehouse of universal riches and abundance.

**6. After you have invoked this dynamic magnetic whirlpool for obtaining large sums of money, sit and cut out five pieces of paper, the size of a dollar bill.** Now write in the four corners of this paper the figure $10,000. Then add these up and count aloud up to $50,000. Do this exercise several times, so you will increase the psychic whirlpool of power through your emotional intensity. Then put the pieces of paper into a box

marked "Deed to my Dream Home" and several pieces of paper
marked "Stock Certificates." Then write down on each stock
certificate the name of some stock that you can get from the
financial columns of your daily paper. Also put into this Treasure Chest a piece of simulated gold, a pearl, diamond, ruby,
emerald, or sapphire. These become the magnetic symbols of
the real things you want to buy with money.

**7. After you have built your Treasure Chest, go to it every
night, just before going to bed, and go through it and create a
psychic whirlpool of desire.** See the money as coming to you;
visualize yourself having the land or home you want; see
yourself having the jewels, or other objects of value. See the
slips of paper marked $10,000 and make your claim on the
riches of the universe. In this way you are creating an invisible
magnetic force that will work through your higher psychic
centers, driving you in the direction of the things you have
magnetized.

**8. Very often you can use your higher psychic centers
through clairvoyant dreams that actually reveal how you can get
the money you desire.** Sometimes, when you have programmed
your psychic centers to reveal things to you about money and
possessions, your higher psychic mind will actually project a
dream in which something will be revealed that might bring you
the money. The reason that we do not always contact this
higher psychic mind while awake is that the conscious mind
stands in the way. It does not want to believe in things that are
not apparent, so it puts up defenses. While you are asleep, this
doubting Thomas of a conscious mind is removed from the
scene and only the higher, subconscious mind is on duty. It is
through this mind that you receive psychic and clairvoyant
impressions.

When you go to bed at night, program this higher mind.
Say a positive statement like this one, or make up your own:

I now ask guidance while I sleep for a clairvoyant dream or
psychic guidance to the making of my fortune. Show me

where there is hidden money, or give me an idea that can bring
me $10,000 or more. I ask for intuitive guidance through my
higher psychic mind centers to where and how I can come into
large sums of money.

## POINTS TO REMEMBER

1. A man got a psychic hunch to invest in a stock that
   brought him the beginning of a million-dollar fortune.
2. Train your higher psychic centers to build a psychic
   whirlpool for attracting riches and abundance.
3. Program your higher psychic mind with desires for
   business, money, creative talents and ideas that can
   make you rich.
4. A woman used this system for creating a psychic
   whirlpool and was guided to entering a cake baking
   contest where she won the sum of $5,000.
5. Create the psychic whirlpool through meditation and
   magnetic statements that stir your psychic centers into
   action.
6. Be psychically guided to obtaining the car you desire,
   the sums of money you want, or other conditions in
   your life, through your higher psychic centers.
7. A woman and her husband were able to create the
   psychic whirlpool and attract the following sums of
   money: $1,000, $5,000, and $20,000. They used this
   to attract a white Cadillac car!
8. A woman was able to draw into her magnetic circle a
   piano that helped her double her income as a music
   teacher.
9. A young man used the psychic whirlpool to attract the
   sum of $20,000, with which he went into a successful
   business.
10. Build your Psychic Treasure Chest and put into it your
    psychic demands for $50,000 or more, your deed for a
    dream home, stocks and bonds valued at thousands of

dollars, and precious jewels like diamonds, rubies, emeralds and sapphires.

11. Build your future fortune by creating a psychic and magnetic whirlpool with $10,000 bills that you create out of paper. You can build any fortune from $10,000 to $1,000,000 using this magnetic whirlpool of psychic energy.

# 15 SCIENCE-OF-SUCCESS SECRETS TO MAGNETIZE WEALTH FOR YOU

# 13

There are certain basic rules that must be followed if you wish to magnetize wealth and success. Making money is as much of a science as is engineering or architecture. If you wish to build a future fortune you must follow these 15 science-of-success secrets that thousands of successful men and women have followed to achieve fame and fortune.

In this chapter you will be shown how to use these science-of-success secrets to magnetize your mind and build a habitual pattern of success and riches.

In formulating these 15 science-of-success secrets, I have checked on the lives of more than 10,000 people in our modern industry, as well as cases throughout history, to find out what made these people successful, and wealthy.

**Success Secret No. 1: Have a master motive in back of your life to achieve riches for some specific purpose.**

To pinpoint your master motive ask yourself the question: What do I want money for? The answer to that question will determine your master motive.

If your answer is: I want money so I can go to night clubs, drink and dissipate and be lazy, with no responsibilities or cares, you will find that this is not a sufficiently strong master motive to make you a great success.

If your reply to that question is: I want money so I can give my family a better home, educate my children and give them financial security for the future, you will have a more powerful master motive and the chances are you will achieve riches and success.

There are six basic master motives that you can use to give you a stronger impetus in the direction of fame and riches.

A. A desire to help your family. To live in a better home, to send your children through college, to provide them with health, happiness and future security.

B. A desire to increase your mental gifts and talents, so you may better help others.

C. A desire to help the sick, the poor and underprivleged, so they may have better opportunities to achieve fulfillment.

D. A desire to raise the living standards of the world through education, science and industry. The wealthy men of the past and present often form foundations to do research in science that can better help humanity Some of these are the Rockefeller, Ford, and Guggenheim Foundations.

E. The desire to banish war and bring peace to the world. Nobel made millions through munitions. When he saw the death and destruction brought about by war, he established the Nobel Peace Prize to be given yearly to the man or woman who did the most to bring about peace.

F. A desire to serve God and bring spiritual progress and unity, brotherhood and better racial relations to the world.

This is the type of master motive which is the highest, and often makes a person a great personal success, as in the case of Dr. Schweitzer, but does not always lead to great wealth. It often leads people into the ministry and the healing arts, and they become successful and sometimes wealthy. Dr. Norman Vincent Peale made a fortune through his book, *The Power of Positive Thinking* and Billy Graham, the Evangelist, is doing great good, but also making money while he does it. Katherine Kuhlman, the spiritual healer on national television, is helping thousands to a better and healthier way of life, but she is also making a financial success.

**Success Secret No. 2: To know your work or product so well that you can utilize this knowledge to give your customers the best service or product they can obtain anywhere.**

It is the person who has a magnificent obsession who makes the greatest success in life.

The artist that loves to paint does not think of the money he is going to make through his art. He is simply dedicated to bringing greater beauty to the world and perfecting his art.

The writer who enjoys his work will write better stories or articles than one who considers his work drudgery.

When you perfect your talents or refine your products, and give the best services you can to the public, they will reward you with patronage, fame and fortune.

Each day, before you begin your work, read a little slogan that you write on a filing card: "Today, I shall strive to give my best to every customer who comes into my place of business."

Take specialized courses to help you understand your work or product better. Subscribe to special trade journals that will keep you posted on the latest developments in your line of work and advise you about new products or new techniques.

**Success Secret No. 3: Build your own powers of mag-**

netism and persuasion so you can influence those you
contact in business.

Emerson once said, "What you are speaks so loudly that I
cannot hear what you say." It is true that your outer personality, your expression, your voice, your grooming and way of
dressing all have an effect on people. Strive always to be
well-groomed and dressed in a conservative fashion that con-
forms to others in your line of work. If you want to wear your
hair long and have bizzare clothing, this is fine, if you are in a
profession such as music, where it is the present style. However,
if you want to be a successful lawyer, doctor, or businessman
and wear shoulder-length hair, a scraggly beard and Levis, you
will soon find yourself isolated socially and businesswise. To
elicit confidence of his clients, a stock broker should look like
an investment counsellor, not like a character out of a movie.

Strive to cultivate your voice so it is pleasant and low-
pitched. Work on your expressions before a mirror, carefully
avoiding a perpetually gloomy or worried expression. The best
expression to wear is one of confidence and happiness, with a
slight smile, without necessarily opening the lips. This is the
expectant, radiant countenance that gives people confidence in
you and makes them feel happy, If you frown and look gloomy,
this will affect your potential customer and make him give his
money and business to someone who can show a happier
expression.

**Success Secret No. 4: Learn to let money work for you,
and establish credit early so you can borrow money to go
into your own business.**

Seldom has any person ever made a great fortune by working for a salary for someone else. Big money generally comes to
those who are able to raise capital and finance their own product or their own place of business.

To be able to borrow money means you can expand your

business when you want to and increase your productivity of your product to fit many wide markets.

To establish credit early in your career, obtain a personal loan from a bank. To do this you will need a steady job and good character references. When you get a small loan of $1,000 or so, make it a point not to touch that money, but pay it back as agreed, with interest. Then borrow a larger sum of money, and be sure that you do not risk it, but pay it back also in the proper time limit. When you have once established your credit with your local bank and they know you pay your debts, you are then ready to borrow the larger sum you need to go into your own business.

**Success Secret No. 5: Find out what it is that people need and then work to fill that need.**

Basically there are certain needs that all people have in common and it is in these fields that the greatest fortunes have been made. These are:

A. Food. This is one of the biggest industries in the world. This also includes restaurants, wholesalers, processing plants and retail outlets.

B. Clothing. This includes everything from designing clothes to manufacturing   and distributing the finished product. Many great fortunes have come through the clothing industry.

C. Shelter. This includes contracting, building, selling and subdividing land. The greatest fortunes in the world have been made through real estate investments.

D. Household furnishings. This includes furniture, refrigerators, vacuum cleaners, washing machines, and all the various articles that a modern home requires.

E. Education. This includes not only colleges and special institutions, but vast libraries, book publishers, magazines and newspapers, as well as mail order courses. Fortunes have been made in this field.

F. Beauty and adornment. This includes jewelry, cosmetology, the cosmetic fields, reducing salons, and all products that cater to beauty. It could also include interior decorating.

G. Repair and maintenance of home furnishings.

H. The automotive trades and related oil industry, tires, garages and maintenance of cars.

I. Entertainment and pleasure. This includes telev ion, motion pictures, stage, and travel agencies. Many great fortunes have been built in this special field, including some of the great movie fortunes.

J. Supplying people's spiritual needs. Some of the greatest concentrations of wealth are to be found in some of our modern churches. Their tax-free incomes permit them to build huge reserves of money that benefit those associated with their organizations.

K. The professions of medicine, law, engineering, and architecture require college training and if you choose one of these professions you will be generally assured of success. It was found that 65% of all college graduates succeed in their chosen professions.

When you have selected the field in which you can excel, prepare yourself by taking special training to fit you for success in your chosen vocation.

**Success Secret No. 6: Build contacts socially with important people in your community.**

Your success will come to you through other people. Choose the leaders in your church, your club, or your community functions, and then try to get to know them. This type of social growth takes time but it is well worth working on, for through these contacts you increase your ability to sell your products or your services in the future.

It is also through these social contacts with rich or influential friends that you can enlarge your group of friends. A woman who is an excellent hostess generally can make her husband a big business success if she cultivates the right people in her community.

One instance that I know of is a woman who married a man who was not too sociable. He was trying to make a success in his law practice in a new city where they moved after their marriage. The wife managed to get an introduction to a leading judge at a social function. She invited him and his wife to come to dinner at their home. There over cocktails and dinner, this charming woman magnetized the judge and his wife. The husband was later given a very important contact with a big law firm that helped him establish himself permanently in his law practice. The judge naturally thought of him and his wife when the chance came for recommending a young attorney for the big job with the law firm.

**Success Secret No. 7: Utilize the things you now have, and do not waste the substance of life; this means your time, your money, and your life energy.**

Too many people throw away golden opportunities for success by thinking that their success lies in some place other than where they now are. They fail to take advantage of the wonderful opportunities all about them, and they sometimes do not use the money, time or energy they now have to advantage.

I know a young man who is striving to make a success in his career as a carpenter. He told me recently in a personal consultation that there simply are no good opportunities for him to make a fortune in his work. I asked him how he spent his spare time and he told me that he watches television two or three hours every night. On Saturday nights he and his wife go bowling with friends. Sunday is a lazy day and he lolls around the house, and if there are any sports on television, he spends two or three hours rooting for his favorite teams. He often sits up late at night to watch a movie or the late-night talk shows, and then invariably he does not get enough sleep and gets off to work in a bad temper, and is exhausted before nightfall.

When I asked him how much time he spent each day thinking of becoming a success or making extra money, he seemed surprised at my question. I then explained to him that in the hours he wasted every week he could be learning a new trade, or discovering some new ideas that might make him a fortune in his own trade.

**Success Secret No. 8: Act the part of a successful and rich person.**

In psychology this is called the art of personification and it means that you imprint your subconscious mind with the thought you want to express to the outer world.

If you go through life thinking and acting the part of a failure, it will project in your personality and people will automatically think of you as being a failure.

To build this outer facade of success and riches, program your subconscious mind each morning before you go to work, or start your day's activities by saying the following subconscious energizer at least five times:

> I now take on the aura of a successful person. I project confidence in my personality, my voice and the words I use. I own the universe and all therein, therefore I am already rich. Today will be my most successful day.

Occasionally go where rich people congregate and try to take on the atmosphere of success. You can attend art galleries and social functions where you can sometimes mingle with successful men and women; try to take your vacation somewhere that rich people will be. This enhances your own aura of success.

I told this to a young lady in New York, who was lonely and wanted to increase her good through a suitable marriage. I told her to go on a vacation cruise on a ship to the Caribbean. There she mingled with many wealthy people. One night in the lounge she met a good looking young man who asked her to dance with him. She fell in love with him and before they returned to New York City, he had proposed marriage to her!

**Success Secret No. 9: In the life of every successful person that I studied I found they used the power of concentration and visualization for achieving fame and fortune.**

I call this the magnificent obsession. If you can concentrate your mind power on the thing you want more than anything else in the world, this becomes a subconscious driving force that is like an obsession. Think, talk, concentrate on the work you enjoy doing and the success you desire. In this way you will create a dynamic subconscious power that will project your inner subjective dream of success to the outer world, making it a glowing reality.

To enhance your powers of concentration and visualization look up the history of some of the world's great achievements that required intense concentration over a period of years. This will help you realize that your own life foundation must be solidly built if it is to endure and be a monument to riches and success.

**Success Secret No. 10: Cultivate the quality of resourcefulness.**

There may seemingly be no chance for you to improve yourself or make a bigger income than you now have, but if you cultivate resourcefulness you will find new opportunities lying undiscovered all around you.

A young lady I know worked on a full-time job as a secretary. She wanted to make more money but had no other sources of income. One day she passed a wholesale leather goods place. She was curious to see what they manufactured and upon inquiry she found they made excellent women's handbags out of an imitation leather that looked like the real thing. They came in all colors. She was so fascinated that she put the idea in the computer of her mind for future use.

She bought one as a sample, telling the salesman she wanted to investigate the possibility of handling this line of goods. At her office the next day she prominently showed her beautiful white bag. The other girls all asked her where she bought it, and when she saw their interest her subconscious flashed the thought: Why don't you buy some bags and start selling them to your co-workers in the office?

She did exactly that, and she made $100 on her first day! From this simple idea she began to handle this line of merchandise, selling to her friends and acquaintances during evenings, Saturdays, and holiday weekends. She was soon making as much money in this spare time way as she made in her weekly salary.

> **Success Secret No. 11: Daily cultivate the money habit, by thinking about money, being aware of its value, and handling it with a consciousness that it represents possessions, power and security.**

Treat money with respect; count the money in your purse each day, so you know how much you have. Put the big bills first, followed by the smaller denominations. Keep the face side of the money facing in the same direction. Every time you spend a dollar, mentally bless it and send it on its way to do great good.

Learn how to budget your money by having small envelopes into which you put the various amounts you can spend that week for different needs. This gives you a sense of order and makes you aware of how much you are spending.

Magnetize your money by concentrating on the things you desire in your life and which money can buy. You will make your mind a money magnet by projecting this desire to your daily life. See the color TV set in your living room; visualize the new car in your garage; mentally project the new house you want to own; see your children going to college and getting a good education. As these dreams are projected in your mind, they will set up overtones in your conscious and subconscious minds, which will react on your sympathetic nervous system, driving you to do the things that will make the money you desire and need.

**Success Secret No. 12: Use the dynamic law of transmutation to convert your ideas into outer success and riches.**

Make out a list of your negative mental qualities. To transmute the negatives into positives you will be turning the minuses into pluses. Your list might look something like this.

*Negative*
Laziness
Spendthrift
Lack of concentration
Waste of time
Gambling
Procrastination
Feelings of inferiority
Habits of fear and worry

To use the law of transmutation and change the negatives into money-making positives, take one of these minuses each day, and cultivate the mental habit of turning it into a positive quality.

**Laziness.** Make yourself do something that you hate to do and which has developed into a habit of laziness. This might be answering your mail, or paying your bills, or visiting a relative you dislike. When you overcome the inertia that keeps you from doing things, you will be developing the opposite habit of action that can actually make you successful and rich.

**Spendthrift.** If money goes through your fingers like

water, make up your mind you will go as long as possible without spending a cent. When it is necessary, of course, you should spend money. But make it a habit to hold out something each week from your salary that you can put away in savings. You will soon build habits of thrift to counteract this negative.

**Lack of concentration.** On this day make yourself practice concentration on things you are doing, especially on money matters. Concentrate on making money; see other people giving you money; project the business ideas you have in your work or business.

**Waste of time.** Do something useful on this day, something that can convert time into money. It may only be learning something useful you can use in your business, or it can be a new word, or working on self-improvement so you can cultivate a more magnetic or charming personality. *Time is money.* Make this your slogan for this day and write it on a card that you can see several times a day.

**Gambling.** You may not have this negative fault, but if you do, realize that you cannot get something for nothing. Gamble only on sure things, and don't risk money on get-rich-quick schemes.

**Procrastination.** If you have the habit of putting things off until another time, do something about it now. Change this into the habit of taking care of today's problems at once. If you hate to answer letters, make it a point to answer them the moment you receive them until you break this habit. If you plan to take a course in evening school but keep putting it off because you are too busy doing other things, realize that this course of study may bring you financial security in the future. Put up a card over your desk saying *Do It Now* to remind yourself that action in the immediate future will secure your more distant future with security and financial growth.

**Feelings of inferiority.** Transmute this into a sense of your true value. Appraise yourself and your gifts carefully. Write down all your good qualities and then realize that you have nothing to feel inferior about. Feelings of self-consciousness and inferiority are usually built in childhood. Go back over your early years and see what contributed to this defect and then set to work to correct it. Study self-help books, practical psychology, and improve your mind and personality, and soon you will have a sense of your true value and will overcome any feelings of inferiority.

**Habits of fear and worry.** Worry and fear go together. Rationalize your fears and worries. If you fear poverty and worry about your bills, do something constructive each day to help you earn more money so you can get rid of your debts. Then your mind will be free of worry and fear. If you have emotional problems that worry you, seek advice from an expert in that field. Fear and worry erode the mind and short-circuit your energy. Natural concern over problems is *not* worry, but if you do something about solving those problems you will overcome tendencies to worry.

**Success Secret No. 13: Utilize the dynamic law of action in your life to project your golden ideas into the realm of reality.**

An idea that you want to make more money and have a fortune in the future can never bring you the fulfillment of your dream, unless and until you take that first step towards your goal through action.

A young man came to me once in Los Angeles for counselling. He had been in the Vietnam war and had been discharged. He wanted to complete his education and become an engineer, but he couldn't afford to go to college. I advised him to check with Veterans' Administration to see if he was not eligible for tuition aid. He made a simple inquiry and found that he could indeed get a complete college education under the Veteran's bill. If he had not taken that action he would have remained uneducated.

Another case in point was a widow who was barely able to get along on the small income she had. I advised her to check with social security and see if she was not entitled to higher benefits. She simply made a telephone call and discovered that she could draw widow's benefits that amounted to a substantial monthly increase!

**Success Secret No. 14: Learn to use the subtle art of super-persuasion to influence people to help you get money.**

I once knew a young man who made up his mind at the age of 18 that he would get a dollar out of some person each day. Sometimes he received equivalent values, not always the money. But working on this theory, by the time he was 24 he owned three used car lots in Los Angeles and was making as much as $50,000 profit a year!

Each time you meet a person in business, mentally project the thought: You are going to give me money. You will buy my product. You will not be able to say "No" to me.

Cultivate the persuasive voice when trying to sell to others. Lower your voice to the lowest note you can talk on and then, using this as a base, vary your tones up and down the scale about four or five notes, always returning to the lower note. This will give you a hypnotic and compelling voice that others cannot resist.

**Success Secret No. 15: Learn to use one of the most valuable commodities you possess if you want to win people and get them to buy your products or your services.**

This is a pleasant smile. Stand before a mirror and study your face when you frown. See how unpleasant it makes you look. Now change it into a smile. See the difference! When you approach a person to get something out of him like an order, a job, or a contract, keep saying to yourself: You're going to like me. I like you. I want to help you. Mentally project a golden line from your forehead to theirs, attaching it to them, and then gently pull this golden line up in the middle, feeling you are drawing the person closer and closer to you. In this way you will actually be projecting your mental magnetism to the person, and he will feel a strange, unaccountable feeling of liking you and wanting to help you.

Do not smile constantly but learn to keep a pleasant expression on your face. If you have difficulty in doing this, practice before a mirror until you are able to keep a smile on your face, with your lips closed, giving you a perpetually pleasant facial expression. People respond to those who smile often, and they tend to stay clear of those who look perpetually severe and who frown or look worried.

## POINTS TO REMEMBER

1. Money-making is a science that you can master and use to increase your fortune and bring you financial security.
2. The master motives have brought millions of dollars to world-famous people of the past and the present, and you can use them to magnetize more money.
3. Use the six basic master motives that rich people have utilized to build fortunes of millions of dollars.
4. Build your powers of magnetism and persuasion so you are better able to influence those you meet socially and in business.
5. Let money work for you by establishing credit with a bank early in life and using it to increase your fortune.
6. There are 11 basic things that people need and which you can use as a guideline to bring you money success.
7. Know the right people and how they can help you build your own business success.

8. A woman built success for her lawyer husband by deliberately cultivating the acquaintanceship of a judge she met at a party.

9. Utilize the things you now have and not waste money, time or energy, giving you more dynamic power to achieve success.

10. You can use the art of personification to make you appear to be a rich and successful person.

11. The ability to concentrate and visualize your success is a determining factor in the achieving of fame and fortune.

12. Building the right money habits daily and learning how to magnetize money by concentrating on it can help you become rich.

13. Use the law of transmutation to turn your negative mental forces into positive success.

14. You can use the art of super-persuasion and a smiling personality to win friends and make them want to help you become rich.

## 20 MAGNETIC MONEY ENERGIZERS THAT CAN TURN YOUR THOUGHTS INTO GOLD

# 14

**E**verything that has ever been created by man was first a mental image. This includes all the buildings, transportation, clothing, ornaments such as jewelry and home decorations, food processing and conserving, television and radio, airplanes and automobiles—all these things were first held as mental images and then released to the outer world through creative action.

Your mind can turn your thoughts into the shimmering gold of success by using 20 simple magnetic money energizers. These help align your conscious and subconscious minds, forming an unbeatable team that can win fame and fortune in the game of life.

You can program your mind each day with magnetic money energizers that will act upon your subconscious mind and drive you to do the things that make you successful and rich.

If you have been negatively programmed by education, by your parent's negative suggestions, or by the thought that you are limited because of heredity or environment, you will break that mold of negativity and supplant it with these positive magnetic energizers for riches and abundance.

## HOW TO USE THE 20 MAGNETIC MONEY ENERGIZERS

First read over the entire list of Magnetic Money Energizers. Grasp the meaning of each programming statement. Realize that under the law of action and reaction you will be programmed to react to certain mental commands you will give your subconscious mind.

The best time to do this mental programming is at night, just before you go to sleep. Read the entire list through once only and then go to sleep, confident that these magnetic energizers are working in your subconscious mind all night while you sleep. They are being programmed into the sympathetic nervous system. When you have done this exercise for a period of two weeks, they will have become a part of your automatic habit patterns of thinking and acting, and you will be guided by your subconscious mind to do the things that can turn your thoughts into the gold of success and riches.

> 1. I now imprint my subconscious mind with the will to succeed, to become famous and rich. I project my golden ideas in a radiant stream of mental and physical energy that can magnetize and attract money, possessions, power, friends, and success in every department of my life.

Whenever you want to activate this particular magnetic money energizer you need only use the two words of dynamic action *I imprint,* and you will flash the entire message to your subconscious mind. This process is similar to the programming that is done on a computer. When you want certain facts released from the computer, you punch a certain key and it automatically triggers all related data pertaining to the subject you wish information about.

Several times a day you might release this magnetic money energizer by thinking or saying the key words *I imprint.*

2. I invoke the law of the harvest and know that there are riches and abundance in the universe which are rightfully mine. The universe teems with treasures and I now attract my share of money and possessions.

The key words to trigger this magnetic energizer are *I invoke.* Think or say these two words whenever you want to use this energizer.

A man of 45 came to my lectures once and told me after the lecture that he considered himself a failure. He had two children and could never give them a college education. He lived in a small, crowded apartment, and saw no chance of ever buying his own home. He complained bitterly, "It sounds good when you tell us to go out and conquer the world and become rich, but how can we ever compete with Rockefellers, Onassis, and Vanderbilts, who have gobbled up all the wealth and resources?"

This man was suffering from the failure syndrome that keeps millions of Americans from attracting their share of supply and abundance. I told him to activate his mind with positive programming, that there was sufficient wealth to go around, and that no person had a monopoly on money and nature's resources.

Two weeks later this same man sought me out. He told me that he had lost his job and since programming his subconscious mind, as I had told him to, things had gone from bad to worse. "Now, I don't have a job and my savings are dwindling," he lamented. "What shall I do now?"

I then explained to him that his subconscious mind was pushing him out of a limited situation so he would be forced to find a more lucrative position. "A mother bird will push her fledglings out of the nest to teach them to learn to use their own wings and fly," I told him. "Your subconscious mind is now being activated to force you into a situation where you can increase your income and be independent."

Sure enough, two weeks later, he returned and told me that he had gone to a competitive firm who knew of his work, and applied for a position as a manager of a department. Because of his years of experience with his firm, he was given a position as manager of a department at a substantial increase in pay! He grinned as he told me this and said, "I guess my subconscious mind knew it had to push me out of that old rut to give me a chance to try my wings at something new!"

> 3. I elevate my consciousness into the realm of creative ideas and dare to dream big. I realize that I can achieve anything which I conceive and I now expand the horizons of my mind to encompass my own business, more money and greater good in every department of my life.

The key words to trigger this magnetic money energizer are *I elevate*.

Each day strive to program into your subconscious mind some new information about your work. Learn new techniques, study trade journals and keep up to date on the latest sales methods for your product or services. Put into your higher mind centers useful information, wisdom and knowledge that will add to your intellectual growth. You can do this by going to your library and getting books on the lives of great men who have achieved success in their chosen fields. In this way you will be expanding your horizons and adding to your mental and intellectual enrichment.

> 4. I command the higher forces of the universe to bring me fame, fortune, happiness, love fulfillment, and all the good things of life that I desire.

Sometimes a weak and neutral mental attitude will bring a person defeat and disappointment. Fortune favors the bold. Use

your key words *I command* every day when you face challenges
that might normally make you feel defeated and distressed.

A woman I know was brought up to think of herself as
being weak, inferior and incapable of competing with men. She
was told that women were created from the rib of Adam, and
that they were to occupy an inferior position in life.

When I met her in our work she was a timid, shy person of
35 and had never married. She worked as a secretary in a big
manufacturing concern and supported her crippled mother.

I had to recycle this woman's mental programming from
earliest childhood to rid her of all her inferior concepts. Then I
gave her this regimen for training her subconscious mind, told
her to make demands on life and people, and not to accept
second best.

It took two months of hard work to undo the results of 35
years of negative programming. But at the end of that time the
change in this woman was remarkable. She began to dress
differently, wearing more colors, and she fixed her hair in a long
bob that gracefully framed her face, giving an illusion of great
beauty and femininity. She actually began to change from the
first week of her programming.

At the end of the two months period of training and
programming her subconscious mind, she became so confident
that she quit her old job, where she was underpaid, and applied
for a new position as an executive secretary to a very big man in
an insurance company. She got the job at a big increase in
salary. But the programming did not stop there; she had been
given magnetizing statements to attract love and marriage, and
soon she was being dated by salesmen she met. One day Mr.
Right came along and, she told me later, she knew instantly this
was the man who would one day be her husband! A year later
this young lady was married happily and is now on her way to
the fulfillment of her great destiny.

5. I recognize the cosmic law of imagination that shapes and
creates all things from a star to a snowflake. I release the
mental images through my subconscious mind of that which I

wish to project to the outer world, creating for me and mine riches and abundance.

Use the key words *I recognize* to program this entire magnetic money energizer into your subconscious mind. Each day exercise your imagination, and see how many new things you can dream up. Visualize the type of home you want to live in; see the new car in your garage; imagine what it would be like to win a lottery for $100,000; and experience the thrill you would actually receive from such an experience.

6. I build the million-dollar consciousness within my subconscious mind here and now, realizing that each day I use a million dollars worth of good without being aware of it. I am conscious of public parks; they are my estates. I use the buses and subways; they are my limousines and cost many millions. I turn on my TV set and have at my command several million-dollar programs that I can view free. I listen to radio and a million-dollar Stokowski symphony thrills me without cost. I use my public library, with its millions of dollars worth of priceless books and enrich my mind without cost. I go to the art galleries and museums and see history's priceless objects, and they enrich my mind and inspire my soul with beauty. The vast petroleum plants process fuel for my use; the food processing plants and the farmers are busy, by the millions, planting, harvesting and producing meat, eggs, vegetables, coffee, sugar and butter for my body's health and nourishment. I am living like a millionaire! I possess the universe and all therein.

To build this million-dollar consciousness, you simply use the key words *I build* when you want to trigger the awareness of the riches you already do possess. This helps magnetize your mind centers with opulence and abundance so you never feel poor or deprived again.

7. I align my higher mind with great creative thoughts from the minds of geniuses throughout history. I take on their

talents and qualities as I emulate their patterns of thought and action.

If you have a desire to become rich through inventions, study the lives of those who have invented and discovered great things. These might include Benjamin Franklin, Edison, John McCormick, or Leonardo da Vinci, whose creative genius first visualized a flying machine. The Wright brothers, who perfected da Vinci's idea, and made it practical.

If you want to become rich through composing songs, study the lives and works of geniuses in the field of classical and modern music.

If you wish to make your fortune through writing great stories, study the works of the authors you most admire.

If you wish to become a businessman and make a fortune in industry and finance, learn the secrets used by the great industrialists of our modern age.

If you wish to achieve fame and fortune in state, city or government politics, study the lives of our great statesmen, and learn their secrets of success.

If you want to make your mark as a lawyer, doctor, engineer, architect or educator, look up books in the library on the lives and accomplishments of great men and women in your chosen field, and let their philosophies and achievements be an inspiration in your own career

To trigger this magnetic energizer in your subconscious mind simply use the key words *I align,* or *I emulate.*

8. I acculturate my mind to higher intellectual levels, knowing that as my mind is enriched, it will project a sense of value to the outer events of my life and bring me riches and abundance.

To be worth more to the world, and to receive greater rewards and riches, add to your knowledge about the world in which you live. "Knowledge is power." When you know a little something about art, music, literature, psychology, philosophy, religion, politics, industry, finances, and investments, you are better able to raise your level of income and increase your flow of riches. You can keep on studying all your life, adding to your storehouse of knowledge, until you have built the type of mind that can easily manage to attract abundance.

To trigger the preceding programming statement use the keywords *I acculturate*. Repeat this as often as you think of it, until you are able to motivate yourself to go into a process of acquiring true culture.

> 9. I correct all negative and limiting ideas that I may have about money and success. Money is not evil; it can be used for good. Rich people are not all wicked; many help the world with their philanthropy. I now magnetize my mind centers with a desire to attract more money so I can do greater good.

To start the subconscious mind working on this programming statement, simply say the keywords *I correct* several times a day.

> 10. I utilize nature's resources wisely and intelligently at all times. I avoid wasting money, food, time or energy. I realize that there are sufficient resources for all and I now conserve nature's products and try to protect the air, water and forests from pollution and waste. I increase my good when I wisely use the products of the earth and sea.

Today we hear a great deal about ecology and pollution, and we know that man is destroying nature's delicate balance and impoverishing the earth by his carelessness in the use of nature's resources. In your daily life, to enrich yourself, conserve your good; don't waste food, don't throw away goods when there is still use in them. Use the law of conservation, and utilize everything you can in a careful and intelligent way.

To motivate this positive programming statement, simply say the key words *I utilize* several times each day.

11. I release the positive emotions each day that can charge my subconscious mind with energizing power to drive me in the direction of fame and fortune. I express the emotion of faith and it gives me confidence in myself. I project the emotion of expectation and I expect my good. I charge my mind with the emotion of intense desire for money and possessions, and I attract these things. I radiate joy in my personality, and I attract friends who help me achieve my goal. I dwell in the positive emotion of love and bless everyone I meet.

You can release this subconscious programming statement by simply saying the key words *I release* several times a day.

12. I change the limitations set on me by birth, heredity, education and environment. What others have done I also can do. I can become as rich as others have become.

This positive magnetic energizer will remove the fear from your mind that you may not be worthy of riches or fame because of the lowly circumstances of your birth. Many millionaires in America did not have a college education. They programmed themselves to believe they could be successful by using their minds to acquire adequate knowledge about their work to achieve great success.

To release this powerful energizer in your subconscious mind simply say the key words *I change* several times each day.

A man who was a junk dealer, and who had very little education beyond grammar school, made up his mind he would be a millionaire before he was 40. He began exporting scrap metal to foreign countries after the second world war. Then, in the same ships he used to export his scrap metal, he began to import products from the foreign countries, until he had built a business over 10 years that grossed him $7,000,000 a year. He now lives in a mansion in San Francisco, has a chauffeur-driven limousine and hobnobs with the socially elite. His money has removed all barriers created by his early environment and lack of education.

> 13. I inspire my mind to high levels of idealism, truth and honesty, knowing that money is a responsibility. I shall do good with my money, helping those who need assistance, and evolving the world to higher levels of civilization.

You can release the power of this money energizer by repeating the key words *I inspire* whenever you want to invoke the principles of idealism, truth and honesty in your life. I have found, upon research, that most wealthy people accumulated their fortunes by hard work and they were generally honest and high-principled. Most of the men who have made great fortunes have generously endowed charitable organizations or foundations, which have continued to help the public long after the donors were dead.

> 14. I express faith in myself, my talents, my country and my God, knowing that with faith I can achieve all things. I magnetize my mind with the magic power of belief, and this spiritual contagion now spreads to every person I meet, causing them to believe in me and my works.

To release this magnetic energizer use the key words *I express* or *I believe.* Repeat it several times daily until you have programmed the entire statement of faith in your subconscious mind. It will then work automatically to give you that extra push in the direction of success which can assure you that you will achieve riches and happiness.

> 15. I radiate enthusiasm and joy in my work and my achievements. I know that my mind and body are given extra energy from my subconscious mind when I live in a success atmosphere. I enthusiastically greet each day, and recognize it as an opportunity to achieve greatness, fame and fortune.

Enthusiasm for your daily work helps you overcome boredom and indifference. Be sure you are in work you enjoy and then greet each day with the key words *I radiate*, and you will program a very powerful magnetic money energizer that will create the chemistry conducive to riches and success.

A scientist who won the Nobel prize once said that he owed his success to the fact he had an assistant who awakened him every morning at seven with the enthusiastic remark, "Wake up! There's great work to be done today!" This gave him the spark that ignited his genius for that entire day.

The other five magnetic money energizers I shall give in brief form, and you may use them whenever you feel you need to stimulate your subconscious mind with new creative energy for achieving fame and fortune.

16. I dream the big and impossible dream, having faith that my dream can come true. As man once dreamed he would one day walk on the moon and grow wings that caused him to fly, so too, I now grow wings of the spirit and I reach the highest goals.

17. I recognize my inherent divinity and greatness. I have inherited the universe and all therein by divine right, and I strive to be worthy of this largesse.

18. I dare attempt to scale undreamed heights, to give the world beauty, joy, good, peace and love, and in so doing enrich the world as well as myself.

19. I bless my good and multiply it under the divine law of abundance, and know that as I give out, so too, shall it be returned to me a hundredfold.

20. I thank God for the gift of life, the gift of mind and body, attuned to His light of infinite intelligence and good. I thank him for giving me this resplendent star, called earth, upon

which I ride in golden glory into infinity, joy and spiritual
treasures of peace, love and immortality.

## POINTS TO REMEMBER

1. Your mind can turn your thoughts into the shimmering gold of success by using magnetic money energizers.
2. Negative mental programming leads to failure, poverty
   and unhappiness.
3. Imprint your subconscious mind with the will to
   succeed, to become famous and rich.
4. A 45-year-old man programmed himself to a change of
   jobs at a big increase of salary when he had long
   thought himself a big failure.
5. Use the key words *I elevate* to raise your consciousness
   into the realm of creative ideas and big money.
6. A woman used the key words *I command* to bring her
   out of a 35-year cycle of failure and frustration.
7. You can build the million-dollar consciousness that
   instantly makes you feel, think, act and live like a
   millionaire. You can inherit the universe through this
   simple magnetic money energizer.
8. You can use a magnetic money energizer to reach
   undreamed of creative heights of genius and compose,
   write, invent, paint, or achieve business success
   through the inspiration of great geniuses of history.
9. You can break the mold of negative programming and
   correct all negative and limiting ideas about money and
   success, attracting as much money as you desire.
10. You can utilize the positive emotions of confidence,
    faith, joy and love to give you magnetic money power
    to attract a fortune.
11. A man built a fortune of $7,000,000 a year and now
    lives in a mansion in San Francisco because he learned

how to change the limitations of heredity, education and environment.

12. The magic of faith can energize your subconscious mind and drive you towards wealth, power and success.

13. You can harness five other magnetic money energizers to scale impossible heights and achieve fame, fortune and riches.

# TAP THE PSYCHIC MONEY BANK
# TO BUILD FINANCIAL SECURITY

# 15

There is a mysterious, invisible power in the universe that ties all elements together and makes them operate under the direction of some higher intelligence.

This power resides within you also. It can guide you to do the things that will bring you financial security. It is the telepathic communication that tells the maple tree when to send the sap down into the roots, to prepare for the long, cold, New England winters. It also communicates to the same trees when it is spring, and time to send the sap back up the trunk to the branches and leaves.

Every time this creative intelligence, which man calls God, wants to create a rose, it does not have to draw a new design. The image of the rose already exists in a psychic invisible bank, in vibrations, and it can be invoked each springtime to produce another crop of roses, or apples, or anything else that is desired.

There is a universal genetic bank that this power can also tap when it wants to produce another human being. The genetic pattern is imprinted in the genes and chromosomes of the mother and father. By some strange telepathic communication, the message is flashed, creating a child that will be a certain height and have a certain color hair, eyes and skin.

A psychic power that is so great it can create a human being in nine months time must also be able to create anything else in the universe that you desire.

In this chapter we shall learn how to tap the psychic money bank that exists in the invisible universe to attract to you money, possessions, lands, houses, jewels, furs, stocks, and other things of value that have been given a dollar sign by man, to designate that value.

These physical and material possessions all spring from the earth and operate under the same identical psychic and cosmic laws that produce trees and lumber to build your dream home, as well as the foods to nourish and sustain mankind.

## REGIMEN FOR TAPPING THE PSYCHIC MONEY BANK THAT CAN BRING YOU FINANCIAL SECURITY

1. First, sit in meditation for about half an hour and concentrate all the powers of your mind on money and the things money can be used for. Mentally create a vast cornucopia, showing it filled to overflowing with houses, money, jewels, cars, land, stocks and other things of value. See this cornucopia pouring forth its treasures for your enrichment. This psychic money bank is loaded with good things. It will respond to your higher psychic mind centers when you sit in meditation and ask that it pour forth a stream of riches and abundance for your use.

2. Use this incantation, which could be called a money chant, for the release of the psychic energy that can be turned into wealth through your creative mind centers.

Intone 10 or 15 times each of these money chants:

Money-money—money. I now magnetize a steady flow of money to enrich my life.
$100,000—$100,000—$100,000. I project this sum of money to give me financial security.

Good luck—good luck—good luck. I am now in the magnetic polarity of good luck that takes away all my bad luck in money matters.

Give—give—give. Give me money or money equivalents immediately to help me solve my money problems.

Receive—receive—receive. I open my mind, my hands, my pocketbook and recieve a steady flow of money and other things of value.

3. The next day go into meditation again, taking with you the following questions, which you write on a sheet of paper. These questions are being communicated to your higher psychic centers, and you will receive answers to these questions. The answers may not come in your meditation sessions, but you may suddenly be guided to do something that will bring you the money you are asking from your psychic money bank.

What should I do to get the sum of $5,000 that I need to pay my bills?

What is my real life work and how should I get into it?

How can I open my own business? What business should I go into?

Should I buy this house or this land?

What stocks should I invest in, and when?

Where can I go to make my big fortune?

Show me how to write stories (or you might ask how to paint pictures, invent objects, compose songs, or get business ideas) so I can make a fortune.

Guide me to the making of $100,000 or more to give me financial security.

4. When you have presented this pattern of events you want to be guided to achieve, come out of your meditation and go about your regular activities. The answers to your questions and the psychic guidance to your fortune may come about in a most unusual and unexpected way.

A man who used this method for tapping the psychic

money bank meditated every day for two weeks. He did not receive any immediate answers to his questions, but one day he read an ad for a book that promised he could make a million dollars in real estate.

He thought this might be the psychic guidance he was seeking that could make him rich. He bought the book, followed its advice and enrolled in a night course in real estate. He got into the business, learning how to buy and sell property. He seemed to be psychically guided to the right customers; he seemed to know the very things to say that made his customers buy from him. He sold more houses in that first year in real estate than two other salesmen combined.

Then his big break came. He sold a million-dollar commercial property to a big company, and from the big commission he received, he opened his own real estate office. This man is now on the way to making his first million.

5. Use the law of psychic duplication, which is the creative pattern that nature uses in creating untold wealth in the universe.

The prototype of everything you want to create is already within your mind. When you think of a house, it exists in the fourth dimensional plane of your consciousness. You can psychically duplicate the location of each room, you can plan the windows, doors and stairs with meticulous attention to details. You can mentally see the fireplace where you want it. You can project a nursery for children not yet born. You have the power to psychically duplicate that house you want to live in for the future, and the elements that can make that dream house a reality already exist in the psychic money bank of the universe.

Sit in meditation for at least 15 minutes a day and psychically duplicate everything you want money to do for you.

Get travel literature and psychically duplicate the trip to Europe for your next vacation. As you program the color photos of Spain, France, England and Greece into your psychic centers, they begin to come to life in an invisible psychic or astral plane. The plane or ship that will take you there is already in existence. The money to buy the tickets already is in the dimension of the material world. You will help magnetize that money through this law of psychic duplication.

This psychic realm is the world of fantasia, in which reality is a dream that all humanity is busy projecting on the fourth dimensional plane of consciousness.

A legend from the Far East exemplifies this act of psychic duplication. A king rode forth from his palace gates daily, on his black stallion, at the head of his troops.

A beggar sat at the palace gates one day, and the king tossed him a gold coin and asked, "Why are you a beggar?"

The beggar thought for a moment and then replied: "It is true, your majesty, that by day I am a beggar, but at night, in my dreams I am king. You, your Highness, by day, are a king, but at night, in your dreams, you fear becoming the beggar I am. Who then, is really beggar and who is really king?"

So too, in your dream world you can be anything you want to be and through psychic duplication, you can create the riches and abundance you want to attract. It becomes a reality the moment you invoke this dynamic mystical law. In a short time, you will find yourself duplicating in your everyday, real world, the things that you built in your psychic or astral thought realm.

A woman in our lecture work collected fine china. There was a piece she wanted to complete a certain collection. It was a very rare and expensive piece and she had no idea where she was going to find it. She sat in meditation each day, and projected the thought form of the missing piece of china, with the request to the higher psychic mind that she would be guided to a source that could furnish her with it.

One night this woman went to an auction in Beverly Hills, California, with her daughter. She had no special desire to buy

anything, but something compelled her to go. Halfway through
the auction the auctioneer announced that they were selling the
very big estate of a woman who had died, including her entire
china collection. When they put the individual pieces up for sale
there was the rare china piece that this woman had asked her
psychic centers to guide her to! She bought it for half the price
she would have been willing to pay.

6. Use the secret power of the psychic Money Syphon to
attract money and things of value to you. You can invoke this
mystical power in whatever circumstance you are in life. There
is no need to live in poverty and deprive yourself of the good
things of life.

Nature has given you the power to draw from the earth all
the elements you need to sustain you as long as you live. A bee
instinctively knows how to draw pollen from the flower to
convert into honey for its food. It is using the psychic syphon
to sustain itself.

I once visited a very poor village in Northern Greece. I was
invited by a friend to be guest at one of the villager's homes. It
was a neat, white stucco house, quite different from the
shabby-looking houses on the same street. When I entered the
living room I was impressed by the fact there was a beautiful
crystal chandelier in the living room. The window sills were
made of solid white marble. The house had a very modern
kitchen and a luxurious bathroom, with a 50-gallon hot water
heater. I knew the other homes in the village had only outdoor
plumbing, and no hot water or bathtubs.

In talking to this man, who spoke some English, I admired
his beautiful home and asked how he happened to live in such
luxury, while the rest of his village was so shabby and poor.

He smiled and told me, "I use a Money Syphon to give me
all the things I want."

I thought I was hearing things and I asked him to repeat
the words. Then he told me his secret of the Money Syphon,
which I later named psychic.

This man had five sons. He worked hard on his small tobacco farm to bring up his family. He dreamed of one day possibly going to some other country where there would be better opportunities for him and his family. His wife had died and with the aid of a sister, he had brought up all five sons.

From the time his children could talk, he planted the ideas in their minds that they must emigrate from poverty-stricken Greece to other countries where they would have more opportunities for success. Soon his children were all grown up. One of them emigrated to Australia and found work. Two went to Canada, where they made their homes and got married. One went to Germany and found excellent work and good pay in a factory and the other one went to New Zealand and found work on a ranch, where he soon became foreman. All the boys were a success in their new homes.

Then, with a twinkle in his blue eyes, the old man said, "Each month my five sons send me $50 each, and sometimes at Christmas and my birthdate, extra money. With this $250 a month here in this poor country, I can live like a king. You see," he continued with a big grin, "My Money Syphon works for me all the way from Germany, Australia, New Zealand and Canada!"

It was in that moment of illumination that I realized God has given everyone of us a psychic Money Syphon which works to bring us whatever we demand of life.

Consider for a moment the breakfast that you have every day, and which you never think of as a miracle. Here you see the principle of the psychic Money Syphon at work. On that table you will have coffee from Brazil. Hundreds of people worked to raise the coffee, pick the crop, market and process it. Hundreds more loaded it on ships and brought it to the market, where you bought it.

The eggs you have for breakfast were laid by some chicken on a farm, tended by people you do not know. The bacon had

to be raised, cured and shipped to be on that table to go with
your eggs.

The sugar for your coffee was cultivated by hundreds of
workers in the beet fields of Colorado, or the sugar cane fields
of the South or Hawaii. The toast you have with your breakfast
is from wheat that was planted, harvested and processed by
farmers you do not even know. This formidable legion of
workers formed a perfect syphon to bring you the simple
breakfast you have always taken for granted every day of your
life. And if you have fried potatoes or cereal for breakfast, this
becomes another invisible syphon from Idaho and the grain
from Kansas or Nebraska.

Your psychic Money Syphon is always working for you, if
you only realize it. To go from a simple breakfast to other
things of value, such as a home of your own, a car, a color TV
set, jewelry, fashionable clothes, and luxuries of travel all over
the world, you simply increase the power of your mental desires
that create the psychic Money Syphon.

To do this, sit quietly in meditation each day, and send
out invisible lines of thought to the areas you want to syphon.
See these lines as fishing lines, with the things attached to them,
and then mentally draw them into your center of consciousness,
saying the following statement to yourself:

> I now create the psychic Money Syphon, which draws to me
> the things I want in my life. I draw into the center of my
> consciousness the sum of $5,000, which I need to help pay my
> debts. I draw a yearly income in excess of $25,000. I draw a
> new car, furnishings for my home, a color television set, a new
> stereo record changer and other things of real money value.

Whenever you want something, project this psychic Money
Syphon to the outer world, where all these things exist and see
it attached to the golden chord you have projected into the
cosmic storehouse of treasures, and then mentally pull it into

the center of your consciousness. You will then be magnetizing
the money centers of your mind and making them sensitive to
every psychic impulse that radiates from your higher mind.
This, in turn, will guide you to the exact place to go for your
dreams to come true.

## POINTS TO REMEMBER

1. A mysterious, invisible power exists in the universe,
   which can guide you to the attainment of money, fame
   and success when you learn how to use it.
2. You can tap the psychic money bank that is in the
   invisible universe and draw to yourself money, possessions, lands, cars, jewels and other things of value.
3. The money cornucopia filled to overflowing with every
   precious gift may be made to pour a plethora of riches
   and abundance into your waiting hands when you
   know how to invoke this power.
4. Use the Money Chants that will bring you anything
   you desire, including cash from $1,000 to $100,000.
5. Use the secret power of meditation, and ask a higher
   psychic mind to give you advice and guidance for
   getting rich.
6. One man tapped this psychic money bank and sold
   more houses than two other salesmen combined.
7. The law of psychic duplication can be used to mentally
   create images of the things you desire. Then project
   those images to the outer world and make them come
   true.
8 A woman used this law of psychic duplication to
   magnetize something of value she wanted. She was
   psychically guided to the auction where the object was
   up for sale!
9. Use the psychic Money Syphon to attract money and

possessions to you, and never again live in poverty or deprive yourself of the good things in life.

10. This principle of the psychic Money Syphon works in nature, giving all creatures the power to draw to themselves the things they require to survive.

11. A man in a poverty-stricken village in northern Greece used this Money Syphon and attracted a beautiful home with crystal chandeliers, modern kitchen and luxurious bathroom, while his neighbors lived in shabby poverty.

12. You can invoke this psychic Money Syphon to bring you money, security, a beautiful home, and everything you want.

13. You can sit in daily meditation, build this psychic Money Syphon, and make it bring you $5,000 for paying debts and an income in excess of $25,000.

# THE MAGIC OF BELIEVING
# AND RECEIVING CAN START
# THE FLOW OF RICHES TO YOU

# 16

There is magic in believing that you can magnetize and attract riches and abundance. You can invoke the supreme cosmic law of faith by following a few simple precepts which we shall study in this chapter. You can become a receiving station for great good when you invoke this simple law of believing and receiving.

The Bible gives one of the most potent laws for becoming successful and attracting your good in this sentence: "If thou canst believe; all things are possible to him that believeth."

Believe that the universe is teeming with riches and that they were created just for you.

Believe that there are no shortages and that all good exists here and now and can be magnetically attracted to you by the use of faith.

Believe in yourself, your gifts, talents, and your power of mind to draw into your daily orbit of experience the money, possessions and good that you want to receive.

Believe in other people and know that they are eager to

help you when you attune your mind to the wavelengths of riches and supply and abundance. You will start the flow of money in your direction.

Believe in God and know that He created a universe just for you to use and enjoy. You are an heir to a kingdom, and you were born to control and rule over the earth and all its infinite treasures.

One basin in the Amazon alone is filled with 20,000 different species of trees that can be used by man for generations to come. This basin is afloat on a sea of oil, which can run man's industry and motors for hundreds of years.

There is so much gold, copper, tin, iron ore and uranium that it can supply the earth's needs for generations.

One forest in Russia is 3,000 miles long, and has enough lumber and other building materials to build a home the size and beauty of the White House for everyone. Why, then, are people living in ghettos with insufficient housing?

The money lost on one battleship in Pearl Harbor was sufficient to bring water from the Pacific, desalinate it, and bring it to the deserts of Arizona, New Mexico and Nevada and make them a flowering paradise.

On one day in California I saw them burn tons of oranges, eggs, milk and potatoes to keep the prices high!

All these things are treasures! God has given us riches and abundance but man's ignorance, selfishness and hatred have kept him from utilizing this paradise which was created for man's good. When we plow under crops and kill pigs and other cattle to create an artificial shortage, we will naturally create recessions and inflation and all the evils that go with misuse and abuse of God's goods.

## REGIMEN FOR USING THE MAGIC OF BELIEVING AND RECEIVING TO START THE FLOW OF RICHES TO YOU

1. Begin each day with an expression of your faith in the

power that can make you rich. Say the following success motivator at least five times before you start your day.

> I have faith in the power of my higher mind to make me rich. I believe there are sufficient riches for all. I now magnetize my mind centers with the magic power of faith and attract to me my greater good.

2. To give you greater faith in your power to magnetize and attract riches and things of value, make a money inventory of the valuable things you may already have and which you do not count as riches. These things are your money assets. Have faith to know that as you have attracted these things of value, so too can you increase that faith and double and triple your income and your worldly goods.

3. Each day have faith that you will attract something of value that will add to your financial security, your comfort, or your benefit.

A woman who used this law of faith found that in two weeks she received money equivalent benefits of $100.

A man and his wife did this for one year and found at the end of the year they had actually attracted $5,000 worth of extra value including an excellent nearly new refrigerator, given to him by his brother who was moving to another state. He needed another car for his wife to drive; he bought one from a friend at a saving of $250. A bonus check came to him that year for $500. His wife was given a gift of three expensive gowns by a rich friend, who had only worn them a few times. These were easily worth $200 each when new.

Besides all these unexpected little things, the man's salary was increased by $15 a week, giving him an additional income of $750 a year.

They estimated that from all these extra sources, they had actually received cash value of $5,000 or more in that one year. Now they are expanding their financial horizons to bigger goals for the future.

4. To increase your faith and awareness of money, keep a

large sheet of paper with your money goals for the year written in large print on it. If you desire an extra $5,000, write on that paper: "I DESIRE $5,000 EXTRA THIS YEAR FROM UNEXPECTED SOURCES."

5. If your overall goal in life is $500,000 put that on paper. "MY GOAL FOR FUTURE SECURITY IS $500,000." Realize that such a big goal takes time, and do not expect it all in one lump sum. If you live 50 years of productive life and spend only $5,000 a year, you have already received the sum of $250,000. Most people have a life cycle of 70 to 80 years, and you should be able to easily make $500,000.

6. To activate the magic power of faith in your life, when you want to increase your inflow of money, give something away. The Bible also gives this law: "Give, and it shall be given unto you." Most people take, but they refuse to give. When you give service, you receive money; when you give friendship and love, you receive love in return. Activate your faith in the law of believing and receiving by giving something away each day that is yours. It need not be money, but it can be a kind act, such as telephoning a sick friend, or visiting him. You can send a get-well card if you cannot go to the hospital. Give congratulations, give praise to your fellow-workers when it is deserved, give appreciation to your mate, and show you care each day. If you can give small gifts of money or other things of value, do so, knowing that this is an expression of faith that your good will return to you. Bread, cast upon the waters, shall return, after many days, and your good will always come back to you.

7. To further start the flow of your good when you awaken in the morning, say a short prayer of thanksgiving. We celebrate Thanksgiving only once a year, but every day you should thank God for the blessings of life. Say a short prayer when you open your eyes each morning: "Thank you God, for another day of life and for the bounties you have showered

upon me. I have faith that today shall bring me new and wondrous gifts and adventures in joyous living."

8. Do not be miserly or hoard your money, fearing that you will be deprived of life's blessings. This attitude stifles the flow of your supply and leads to worry and fear, which in turn rob you of the joys of life. By spending money and keeping the channels of supply open, you follow the natural law of the universe. The sun gives of its substance, and never holds back its life-giving rays. The rain blesses the earth and crops grow abundantly. The soil gives us food, lumber, and oil, and life on this earth is sustained. If God stopped giving, there would be no life for any of us. So have faith that your flow of riches will continue and spend what you need to give you and your family comfort and security.

I once knew a man who was terribly worried about his family of three children and his wife. He never stopped talking about the necessity of keeping money in reserve for unexpected misfortunes or tragedies. I saw this man often over a period of 10 years, and every misfortune he prepared for came! His wife became sick, as he always knew she would, and required emergency surgery for a gall bladder removal. The three children each had their separate bouts of illness; two of them had separate accidents, each breaking a leg and an arm, in a period of two years. The man himself finally became a victim of high blood pressure and had a coronary attack. "That which ye fear shall come upon you." When you have faith in your evil, lack and limitation, it comes. If you can turn this into faith in your good, it will also come.

9. Day by day, the manna fell from heaven to feed the children of Israel in their perilous journey out of bondage. Believe that your money supply will be replenished every day and that your needs will be met. Express this faith by preparing to live in a better home or apartment. Keep adding to your store of beautiful furnishings, dishes, silver, and linens. The

old-fashioned hope chest that girls used to create, waiting for their day of marriage, is a good principle to establish in your mind. Build your hope chest for future wealth and supply. Have faith that you will receive the raise in salary, or the better job that will pay more. Put that down payment on the house you want and know that the money will come to pay for the monthly payments, taxes and other expenses. Go into the marriage you want, not worrying about how you'll be able to afford it.

I once knew a couple that were married and wanted children, but they kept feeling that they did not have enough money to afford a family. They had no faith in the future. The husband expected to be laid off his job in airplane construction, and sure enough, he was. He got another job, and still felt that it was a precarious time to bring children into the world. Now, 10 years later, this couple still remains childless. The wife now fears she is too old to have children, and the husband worries about the inflation and costs of educating his children, so they remain frustrated and without the love of a family.

## POINTS TO REMEMBER

1. You can magnetize money and success through the building of faith. This miracle-working power can be applied to riches and abundance in your daily life.
2. Implement your faith in the riches and abundance that are in the universe, and prove that there is more than enough for every person alive, for centuries to come.
3. Man's waste and selfishness destroys his good and brings about recessions and inflation; avoid this waste by applying the law of faith.
4. Learn how to express your faith in your good each day with a simple success motivator, which you repeat five times at the start of each day.

5. Create a money inventory of the things of value you now have and add to it, through faith, the things that you want to attract for the future.

6. A woman used this law and received equivalents of $100 within a very short period.

7. A man and his wife applied the law of believing and receiving and made $5,000 in extra money in one year.

8. To increase faith and awareness of money, have a money chart on which you list the sums of money you want, from $5,000 to $500,000 or more.

9. You can activate the flow of money to you by using the cosmic law of giving; give service, friendship and love, and your life will be enriched and blessed.

10. To increase your flow of riches, each day give thanks to God for the abundance already bestowed upon you. This expression of faith restores the balance between mind, body and soul that is necessary to progress in life.

11. Avoid being miserly or hoarding money in anticipation of future disasters and tragedies. This stifles the flow and sometimes brings the disasters you anticipate.

12. Faith is a day-by-day expression that causes the riches and supply to flow perpetually. Build a hope chest of the mind, and have faith that your good will come to you daily.

# 7 DYNAMIC MONEY MAGNET
## LAWS THAT CAN
## MAKE YOU RICH

# 17

Money responds to universal laws that are as fixed as the stars in their courses. Once you know how these laws work in relation to money, you can implement them in your own life and start the flow of riches in your direction with greater ease than when you are not aware of these laws.

In this chapter we shall explore the seven dynamic money laws that can make you rich. These are not usually given in courses on economics but they are basic laws that must be understood and used, if you want to increase your flow of riches.

A woman I once knew suffered perpetually from a shortage of money. She told me one day, "I just hate money and the whole economic system that capitalism represents. Why can't people just use God's resources without putting a money value on them?"

Then I explained to her that money was only a symbol of something of value, and used only for exchange. Instead of carrying a bag of potatoes to a market place and exchanging it for a calf that someone else had to carry, it was much easier to carry a piece of folded paper called money, and give it to someone for the bag of potatoes or for the calf.

By seeing money as a medium of exchange, I told her, she would realize that its possession was not evil but something desirable. I changed her entire viewpoint about money and when she next saw me she told me that she had now begun to make more money and to use it with a totally different sense of its value.

### THE SEVEN DYNAMIC MONEY LAWS YOU CAN USE TO MAKE YOU RICH

#### No. 1: The law of magnetic attraction

This dynamic law works in the realm of nature. In the spring the sun's rays draw the sap of the trees from the roots up into the branches, where flowers and fruit soon appear.

In the soil a kernel of corn attracts to itself, by this law of magnetism, the elements it needs to form a stalk of corn. When you consider what a miracle this is, you realize that magnetism is the secret, invisible power in back of all life.

Magnetism works in the same way in your mind, to attract to you that which you put into your brain centers. If you negate this force of magnetism and project the repulsion side of magnetism, it will drive people and fortune away from you.

This is one reason why many people live in poverty all their lives. They short-circuit the magnetism of their minds by constantly thinking and talking about poverty, failure, sickness and misery. We attract what we magnetize our minds with.

To strengthen money magnetism in your mind and attract a big fortune, do the following things to build money magnetism:

A. Each day devote time to keeping a money record of all

you make and all you spend. This helps imprint on your subconscious mind some idea of what you are doing with your money.

B. Each time you spend money mentally magnetize it by blessing it and telling yourself it will come back to you tenfold.

C. When you hear people crying poverty, or telling you about how inflation or recession will take your money, mentally affirm to yourself that supply and abundance exist in the universe and that you will always attract what you need.

D. Build money power by studying the lives of those who have magnetized and attracted vast fortunes. Learn how they did it and what they thought and did to achieve their fortunes. You can study the lives of these rich men in the books published about them and carried in your library.

E. Study publications like *The Wall Street Journal, Forbes,* and *Fortune Magazine.* These give facts about industry, finances and investments that might show you how to apply techniques for accumulating wealth in your life.

F. Each day when you start your day, give yourself the following magnetic statement for money:

All day today I am conscious that my mind is a money magnet. I shall be aware of what money is. Money is frozen energy, crystallized ideas, a medium of exchange. I now magnetize money and attract all I need to give me everything I want in life.

G. See money as a symbol of value, but of no value in itself. Do not see it as something to hoard and hold but as something to use intelligently to purchase the things you need in life.

H. Do not love money, but respect money and want money for the good you can do with it.

I. Magnetize your mind with thoughts of money each day

for at least half an hour. You do this by thinking about money, how to make more, how to increase its flow to yourself from others, and how you may obtain money-making ideas from your higher mind centers.

J. Use the money and possessions you now have intelligently, without waste and extravagance.

K. Sit down and write out 10 good reasons why you want large sums of money. Then intensely desire the things you would do if you had money, and you will magnetize enough money to do everything you desire.

### No. 2: The law of reciprocity

If you want to become wealthy and have fame and success, use the cosmic law of reciprocity. Be willing to give something of value to the world for everything you expect to obtain from life.

No one ever gets something for nothing. This is a fallacy that many people have. Gamblers think they will win at Las Vegas or at the race track. They don't realize the odds are against their winning many times.

Even the stock market is a form of gambling, but at least in the stock market you have a chance to hold your stock when it goes down, and wait until it goes up again.

Money obeys this law of reciprocity. The rich rewards of life are given to those who earn them. The soil is ready and willing to give back an abundant crop of wheat, oranges, melons or potatoes, but first it must receive the seeds that will produce these crops. If you withold the seeds, the soil is powerless to give you the things you need to sustain life.

To implement this dynamic money law do the following things:

A. Be willing to give something of value for the money or possessions you are trying to magnetize and attract.

Hilton is worth millions because he uses this dynamic money law of reciprocity. He gives the best service he is capable of giving; he furnishes his places in the best taste; he locates them around the world so travelers may avail themselves of his facilities whether in Istanbul or Hawaii.

Ford has always given value to the public with his cars and this, under the law of reciprocity, has given him a vast fortune. The Ford Foundation is still giving to the public, in grateful appreciation for what the world gave Ford. Before the first Ford died he said, "One day it will be considered a sin for any man to die rich. He will give back his fortune to the world."

Many people who have made millions do this. They endow their money to charitable, educational, or research foundations that benefit millions of people.

B. Each day strive to use this law of reciprocity. Give your time, labor and effort, with the knowledge that you will be paid for your work. But if you try to skimp on what you give, life very quickly will repay you by giving you less and less of material value.

Like the town lazy man, when the farmer approached him with work in a busy season. The lazy man asked, "What will you pay me?"

The farmer replied, "Exactly what you're worth."

The man replied, "I'll be durned if I'll work for that little."

Life does pay us exactly what we're worth, even though we may not believe this.

C. Do everything you can to increase your value to the world, not diminish it. When you leave college and have your diploma, do not sit back on your laurels and think you need never again make any effort and that success will come to you.

Be a perpetual student and keep advancing the frontiers of knowledge, so you can keep up to the modern scene and learn all the latest scientific techniques that you can apply to your own chosen profession.

D. If you are interested in making a big fortune, stop and evaluate what you have to give for this fortune. It does not always depend on the labor you do, for sometimes one idea can make you a million dollars. They say a man is only worth a few dollars a day from the neck down but from the neck up, in the realm of the intellect, he can be worth millions of dollars.

Ask yourself the following questions:

How can I improve the product I am selling and make it better?
What can I do to give better service to my customers?
Am I overcharging for my goods or my services?
Do I try to please people by having a smiling and charming personality so they will come back to me?
How can I make it easier for people to do business with me and not go to a competitor?

A man I once knew had a small concession selling newspapers, cigarettes and magazines in the lobby of a hotel. He had a surly personality and growled at his customers. Soon the guests at the hotel stopped buying things from him and his business got worse and worse, until he was forced to close. He grumbled, "I worked like a slave to serve those people and they didn't appreciate me."

Another man went into the same location, and made a tremendous success of the business. He greeted people with a friendly smile; he learned a few words of French, German and Spanish, so he could greet people in their own language, as this was a big tourist hotel in midtown. This man is making enough money to send his two sons through college. The other man who failed is now on welfare!

### No. 3. The law of supply and demand

The law of supply and demand is an economic factor that is vitally important in any business. Try to get into some business where you believe the demand is going to be greater than the supply and you will soon become rich.

When wheat is in short supply, the price of bread goes higher, and the price of wheat rises, bringing greater wealth to the farmers. We have seen the result of oil shortages recently, and the spiraling prices of gas and fuel oils.

To work with this economic law, find out what fields are going to be in demand, and which are going to be in short supply, and then start to handle the products for which there will be a bigger demand. This requires a study of the current markets and an understanding of the working of this law in business, which many people have used to become rich.

A man I know was in the commodities field a few years ago. He told all his friends to buy up cocoa futures. In a few months time those who bought them made fortunes. The same thing happened with soy beans. If you can be a prophet and know intuitively which fields will be best to invest in, you can make your fortune in the stock market or the commodities markets.

The big businesses of the future are the following: substitutes for coal, oil and gas. Cars that will run on batteries or with steam will no doubt be in demand. Plastics will still be a growing business. Building of homes and apartments to care for a growing population will also be another good business. Furnishings and kitchen and bathroom supplies will also be required for the growing population. All related businesses, such as electrical and plumbing and lumber supplies, will be needed. Road building will take more cement, asphalt, and other related products. Air conditioning, refrigeration, computers . . . all these will be in demand in the future, to meet the growing requirements of an expanding economy. Steel will no doubt come back into its own on the stock market of the future, as the building of subways in big cities continues to meet the gasoline crisis.

There are certain other fields in which you can make a fortune, which will always be in demand—clothing, food, and cosmetics. People will continue to use products in these three categories, no matter if there is a depression or recession. Shelter, of course, is also a necessity, and real estate sales and construction should all boom in the years ahead.

### No. 4: The law of usage

To increase your riches you must learn to use the law of usage intelligently. God has given man everything he will ever need to survive on this planet. But if we waste nature's resources and violate this law of usage, we will soon suffer from man-made shortages. This applies to our food products as well as to our natural resources of oil, coal, steel and other products that come from the earth.

"Waste not, want not" is an adage that applies to this universal law of usage. Use your time wisely and do not waste it on useless pursuits. Waste of time is like throwing money away. You may say you need rest and relaxation, and this is true, but most people waste three or four hours of their precious time every day on television, where they seldom receive anything worthwhile. If one hour a day were taken from TV viewing and put to constructive use learning a new business, a language, or something else of positive value, one could soon achieve proficiency in whatever field he chose.

Waste of money and goods is even worse. You will always have enough of everything if you learn how to conserve what you already have. Many people throw furniture away after a few years wear, when it could be easily upholstered and repainted and made to last a few more years. Use that money for other things that might be important, such as saving to go into a new business or obtaining enough capital to create some product you can put on the market.

E. Knight said of waste: "Waste not the smallest thing created, for grains of sand make mountains, and atoms infinity. Waste not the smallest time in imbecile infirmity, for well thou knowest that seconds form eternity."

### No. 5: The law of the harvest

This cosmic law states that you will receive the crop back that you have planted. The Bible gives it clearly: "As ye sow, so shall ye reap."

If you plant no seed in the garden of destiny in the springtime of life, you will certainly not be able to reap a harvest in the fall. No matter how young or how old you may be, there is still time for you to use this cosmic law of the harvest.

Each day put mental seed into your consciousness of the supply and abundance you want in the future. Concentrate a few minutes of each day on how you can start a bigger flow of money in your direction. Perhaps it can come through extra work; you may have some gift or talent you are not using that you could commercialize on.

Write down on four pieces of blank paper the sums of $1,000, $5,000, $10,000 and $100,000. Then for one week concentrate on the $1,000. Tell your higher mind, "I want to materialize $1,000 extra for my use in the next three months."

When you have grown more confident and have faith in your power to demonstrate $1,000, graduate to the $5,000, and then to the $10,000 and the $100,000. It may not come all at once, but this money magnetizing process will begin to implant in your consciousness a sense of value and your subconscious will gradually release ideas that will bring you the sums you have planted in your higher mind.

Do not be afraid to give more than you receive, for the law of the harvest decrees that whatever you give to life, it must come back increased in value. Some people stint on their services and think by working less they are being clever and getting a salary for little work. Actually, they are cheating themselves, for by robbing others of time or money, we actually rob ourselves. It furnishes the subconscious mind with a deceptive master motive, and the subconscious then releases less creative intelligence and energy, so the person becomes deceptive in other areas of life and cheats himself in love, friendship, talents and character.

A man I once knew boasted how he worked half as much as the others on his job. He found many ways to shirk his responsibilities and throw his work on others. Soon he was called into the front office and shown a record that had been kept about him and his work. The supervisor had been aware of this man's deception and gave him his notice of dismissal. This man grumbled that life was unfair and that he was deserving of something better. Actually, he was a cheat and a thief, for when you steal someone's time you steal his money, and life was getting back at him for his deception.

### No. 6: The law of growth

This law applies to money as well as to other things in life. It is a universal law. In the soil this is known as the law of capillary attraction; the seed is able to attract to itself the necessary elements it needs to grow and evolve.

When you establish what salary you want, what work you wish to do, and how rich you wish to become, you will be using this law of growth in your own life. Somehow you will be able to attract the elements you need to fulfill the destiny you have chosen.

To work this law of growth in relation to attracting riches and abundance, never stop learning and expanding your intellect. Acquire new facts about your business; grow in your knowledge about the world of business and finances. Study books that keep you abreast of the times, especially in relation to money matters.

If you do not have sufficient education to succeed in the field you have chosen, go to night school and take a course that will prepare you for the better job or bigger business opportunity.

A man who came into our work in New York City was in

insurance, but he wanted to go into another field, for which he was untrained. This was fashion designing. He had an artistic and creative mind, so I advised him not to give up his well paying job, but to go to fashion designing school in the evenings. So he enrolled in one of the biggest of such fashion schools in the city. In two years time he was proficient in his new vocation, and when he applied for a job with one of the big fashion houses in women's wear, he qualified. He gave up his insurance office job, and is now making big money in his new profession.

### No. 7: The law of dynamic action

Action is the first law in the universe. It is what keeps the entire universe operating. It also works in the realm of finances and you cannot really become rich until you invoke this law of dynamic action. You may have action in your life now, in the sense of going to work each day and doing your daily tasks with a minimum amount of effort. But this is not dynamic action.

To have dynamic action, there must be consistent effort along one line of activity. The magnificent obsession of your life must be featured prominently each day. You must think, talk and dream about your work. If you can arouse this type of enthusiasm you will be using dynamic action in your thinking. Then the sympathetic nervous system communicates this dynamic action to your nerves and muscles, giving you that type of dynamic energy that is called genius.

Thomas Edison said of genius, "Genius is 1 percent inspiration and 99 percent perspiration." Dynamic action is the force that carries out your ideas in physical form.

D. G. Mitchell said, "There is no genius in life like the genius of energy and industry."

You can become as rich as you want to be, if you use this law of dynamic action in your life and apply yourself with energy, enthusiasm and persistence.

Dynamic action also applies to your money; it must be

made to work for you. This can be done through savings banks, where you earn a certain rate of interest on your money, or it may be done by putting money to work, in what is known as invested capital. A man once invested a few dollars in a street vending ice cream cart. No one would ever think that this was the building of a multimillion dollar fortune. The man never stopped working on his idea to expand and grow and become rich.

Soon he had expanded to three vending carts, and had others work for him. In a year's time he had enough capital to buy a small truck and his ice cream vending was expanded to stores and ice cream parlors.

A man by the name of Howard Johnson needed someone to distribute ice cream to his growing chain of stores. He signed a contract for this man to furnish trucks for this purpose. As Howard Johnson's chain became bigger and bigger, he found he was spending thousands of dollars for the trucks he was leasing. He wanted to own his own fleet of delivery trucks, but he had an iron-clad agreement with the man who had started as a street vendor. Howard Johnson finally bought out this man's contract at a cost of $7,000,000! The ice cream vendor then went into other big businesses where he made millions of dollars.

E.B. Hall said of this dynamic quality of action: "Remember you have not a sinew whose law of strength is not action; not a faculty of body, mind, or soul, whose law of improvement is not energy."

Action produces that dynamic energy which you require to carry you on to fame and fortune.

Each day take some action that will make your goal come closer than the day before. Have an active imagination, and create within your mind the mental pictures of yourself doing great deeds, performing noble actions, and winning high goals. As you mentally activate your imagination you will be adding to your strength and energy to carry out the big goals you have set for yourself.

## HOW TO USE THIS BOOK TO BECOME RICH

In using this book to help inspire you to the achievement of fame and fortune, do not merely read it over once and then lay it aside. Take one chapter each week and apply the principles in that chapter to your life. Make mottoes of some of the instructions given and put them on small filing cards which you can look at several times a day. As you absorb the principles of each chapter, go on to the next chapter, applying the principles given there, until you have mastered them fully.

By the time you have studied the entire book in this way, you will have programmed your subconscious mind with the knowledge given in each chapter, and you will then be able to change your patterns of thought and action in regard to making a fortune. When you have built the new habit patterns in regard to thinking of money as being easy to obtain, you will automatically be guided to doing those things that will make you rich. You will have created a money magnet in your mind that will bring you untold wealth!

## POINTS TO REMEMBER

1. Use the magnetic law of attraction to bring you money and increase your riches.
2. You can use 11 points to increase money magnetism within your mind and attract your riches and abundance.
3. Use the law of reciprocity to bring you fame and fortune.
4. Use the secret power that made a success of Conrad Hilton, Henry Ford and other millionaires, who used the law of reciprocity.
5. A man lost his business by failing to obey this cosmic law; another man in the same location made money by utilizing the law of reciprocity.

6. The law of supply and demand works in economics, and you can use it to bring you riches.
7. A man I knew made a fortune in buying commodities because he studied this law of supply and demand.
8. Choose the big businesses of the future, and make your millions through this dynamic law of supply and demand.
9. The law of usage has made millions for those using it, and it can make you rich, when you apply it.
10. The law of the harvest can be used to bring you a crop of riches and abundance in your future.
11. Plant the seed money in consciousness of from $1,000 to $100,000 and invoke the law of the harvest to bring it to you in the shortest possible time.
12. A man cheated himself out of a fortune by violating this law of the harvest, giving less than he received on his job.
13. The law of growth can bring you money and other treasures when you grow and evolve mentally.
14. One man left the insurance field to study art, and became a big fashion designer through this law of growth.
15. You can use the law of dynamic action to increase your riches and achieve your every goal in the future.
16. An ice cream street vendor, with a pushcart, went from a small business to the building of a $7,000,000 fortune.